By SHEILA OSTRANDER

festive food decoration
FOR ALL OCCASIONS

 STERLING PUBLISHING CO., INC.   NEW YORK

 The Oak Tree Press LONDON AND SYDNEY

DEDICATION

This book is for

Sylvia Link

who originated the idea of the
book and whose generous advice and
encouragement made it possible

and for
Grace and Raymond Schroeder

in affectionate gratitude
for their help

"Festive Food Decoration"
Copyright © 1969 by
Sterling Publishing Co., Inc.
419 Park Avenue South, New York 10016
Adapted from "Food Sculpture and Decoration"
Copyright © 1965 by
Sterling Publishing Co., Inc.
Published in Great Britain and the Commonwealth
by Oak Tree Press, Ltd., 116 Baker St., London W. 1
Manufactured in the United States of America
All rights reserved
Library of Congress Catalog Card No: 75-90812
Standard Book Number 8069-3034 9
UK 7061 2225 9   8069-3035 7

CONTENTS

Before you begin

Sculpt a few vegetables to be the guests of honor at your table! This book includes a whole menagerie of fruit and vegetable animals, birds and wacky creatures to highlight any children's party table. In addition, there's a wealth of bright ideas for garnishing and serving foods, and dozens of novel centerpieces and party favors to boost your rating as a hostess.

Vegetables can be as much fun to carve as wood or soap and they add eye-appeal to all sorts of dishes from hors d'oeuvre to desserts.

You don't have to wait for a special occasion to decorate the table either. Food sculpture can add a charming touch to everyday meals too. Fruit and vegetables in some of the following masquerade costumes are sure to spark any appetite and they add an extra-special touch to the dinner tray for a sick child.

Besides being an ideal rainy day pastime, food sculpture is an amusing game for youth groups at playgrounds, camps or clubs. For parties, give your young guests the makings of a vegetable zoo and let them have all the fun of creating their own party favors. Prizes can be awarded for the most original ones.

A few clever food sculptures on a bake sale counter at a bazaar or fair will not only get attention but will add real sales appeal to the baked goods.

Best of all, these serving ideas and food creations are wallet-wise and most of them take only a minimum of time to prepare from foods around the house. Your own imagination will supply encores to the ideas that follow.

HOW TO CARVE—Some of the projects are more complicated to make than others and require a bit of practice. A beginner would do best to start with the simpler things and work up to the more difficult items. Each of the projects has been made and can be duplicated if directions are followed.

Most of the simpler food carving projects can be done with small scissors or a sharp knife. Even a nailfile or a wire cheese cutter or a lollipop stick can be used.

For the more difficult items it would be helpful to have: a paring knife; a trimmer; a vegetable peeler or a vegetable friller; cookie cutters; a pastry crimper; an egg slicer; a grapefruit scalloper.

Always choose fresh, crisp foods. If vegetables to be carved are boiled for just a few minutes in vinegar, salt and water, it

will make the vegetables a little softer and easier to carve as well as prevent discoloration.

With a soft pencil, trace the outline for your carving on to the vegetable. (If you wish, use a pattern or drawing cut from a magazine. Trace it on to the vegetable by placing a piece of carbon paper under it.) After outlining, rough out the design to block out feet, nose, ears, tail, etc. This will help to get them in proportion. Then with the tip of the knife, cut straight into the vegetable on the outlines. These scored lines form guide lines for carving. Hold the knife as you would to pare, bracing your thumb against the vegetable, and cut towards you, working from the outside to the deepest cuts. Pare off small bits at a time to prevent breakage and gradually work down to the shape you want. Use a potato peeler to smooth off curves.

Should a part break off, it can easily be attached again with a straight pin or a toothpick. Or, to correct a portion of the carving that doesn't suit you, just cut it off and replace it with another piece of vegetable toothpicked in place. Then, recarve the segment.

HOW TO PRESERVE FOOD SCULPTURES—To prevent foods from becoming discolored, the cut surfaces can be rubbed with lemon. Or, the raw, peeled vegetables can be dropped for a minute or so into a pot of boiling water containing a few spoonfuls of vinegar, or lemon juice, citric acid crystals or ascorbic acid tablets. Also the vegetables can be marinated in a vinegar-sugar solution after parboiling. If the foods are not intended to be eaten (such as centerpiece displays), salad oil, glycerine or even castor oil can be poured on to the surface and it will keep them looking fresh.

To prevent some food carvings from shrivelling and also to give them a protective lustre, coat them with shellac or lacquer. A covering of clear, liquid plastic on such things as slices of grapefruit, oranges or lemons that are to be used for decoration only will prevent the juice from dripping and will, in addition, make them glisten and look more attractive.

Another method of preserving sculpted food is to spray it with liquid floor wax or white candle wax. Light a candle and let the wax drip on to the vegetable or fruit until it is completely coated.

Foods prepared in advance for party decorations should be kept preferably under glass in a refrigerator or in some cool place.

Now, let's begin . . .

Fruit Sculpture

APPLES

Apple Piglet

Hold the apple so that the stem is the piglet's tail. Cut four short slices of celery to use as the legs. A round carrot slice is the snout. Cut triangles of carrot to make the ears. Two raisins are the eyes. The piglet can also be made from an orange or peach. If you use one of these fruits, add a carrot shred for a tail.

Clown on a Stick

Insert a plastic spoon or a lollipop stick in an apple and slide a doily on to it to form the clown's ruffled collar. Stick on criss-crosses of marshmallow for the clown's eyes. A maraschino cherry is the nose and his mouth is a wide slice of banana peel, held in place with short toothpicks. Spread cream cheese on top of his head with a knife and arrange it in a shaggy hairdo.

Santa

To an apple add a marshmallow head. With syrup, stick on tiny marshmallows for the buttons and for fur on his suit, as well as his beard. Use raisins for eyes and nose. Draw on arms with food color. A triangle of apple peel is the hat, topped with a miniature marshmallow pom-pom, held on with a toothpick.

Apple Cups

Cut across the apple three quarters up from the bottom. Scoop out the fruit and remove the core. Scallop the edges. Fill with nuts or a Waldorf salad made of apple, celery, nuts and mayonnaise.

Apple Faces
for Dolls

Faces carved from apples seem to have real personalities and look almost lifelike. All sorts of wrinkly-faced characters can be made—Indians, pirates, pioneers and so on.

Peel the apple as smooth as possible and remove the stem. The features can be carved with a small spoon. Cut deep indentations for the eyes and mouth. The apple will tend to shrink as it dries, so make the features slightly larger than the way you will want them to look in the finished product. Carve a large nose, round off the forehead and put a few wrinkle lines into it. Carve ears also, if they will show when the doll is in costume.

Dip the apple in vinegar or lemon juice for a few minutes to prevent it from becoming discolored. Then set it in a warm place to dry.

To make the eyes, use beads or carpet tacks or small round-headed nails. Press the nails into the eye openings and, as the apple shrinks, the skin will form eyelids around the nails.

Make sure the apple is completely dry before you begin to paint on the doll's features. Use real face make-up or

Carve nose, deep slots for eyes and mouth and make cuts in forehead for wrinkle lines.

tempera colors. Bits of rice or unpopped kernels of corn can be inserted to form teeth.

Glue on cotton batting, fur or wool to form beards, moustaches, or doll hair.

A bottle can form the doll's body. Carve a hole in the apple so it fits over the top of the bottle. To make the head fit firmly, wrap the neck of the bottle with strips of cloth and then carefully glue the head in place.

Costumes can be made of doll clothes or crepe paper. Different bottles will suggest various costumes. For instance, a bell-shaped bottle can be dressed as a hoop skirt for a doll.

Cut out arms from cardboard and tape them on to the bottle before putting the clothes on. Add tissue paper stuffing to fill out the clothes if they do not quite match the contours of the bottle.

Wooden legs can be glued to the bottom of the bottle if they are necessary to the costume. Feet or shoes can be made from soap, clay or wood and glued to the legs or to the front edge of the bottom of the bottle.

Sheep

Roll an apple in honey or syrup and then cover it with popcorn. Insert four strong toothpick legs and a puff of popcorn on half a toothpick as the tail. The head is a marshmallow painted with a food color face. Small triangles of marshmallow toothpicked in place are the ears.

BANANAS

Banana Gondola

Slit a banana down the middle being careful not to cut through the skin on the lower side. Leave the banana stock on as the prow of the gondola. The boatman is a stick of celery. Use a piece from the upper end of the celery stalk that has two branches to form the boatman's legs. Toothpick on a partly peeled radish head and draw on features with food color. Two narrow slices of celery are the arms. Hold them in place with straight pins. A long stick of uncooked spaghetti is the boatman's pole. Rest the stick against his shoulder and pin one of his celery arms around it.

Banana
Firecracker

To make a banana firecracker, use a strip of lime peel for the fuse. Make other firecrackers already "lighted" with a cherry for the flame.

Banana Hearts and Flowers

Cut circular slices of banana. Then with a small cookie cutter, re-cut each banana circle into the shape of a heart, or clover, or flower, etc. These attractive banana slices can decorate ice cream, cereals or can be served with cream.

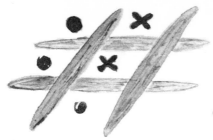

Tick-Tack-Toe

Cut four lengthwise slices of banana and arrange them in a tick-tack-toe pattern. Use shelled nuts for the circles. With scissors cut "X" shapes from pitted dates. All can make a cake-top decoration.

Banana Marshmallow Boat

Fill a banana with a cargo of marshmallows. Slit the banana down to the lower skin but do not cut the skin. Cut out sections of the fruit, and fill the spaces in the banana with marshmallows. Broil until the marshmallows begin to melt.

CANTALOUPE

Also see Melon

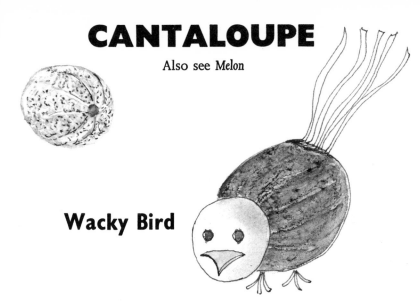

Wacky Bird

Made from a cantaloupe with a lemon for a head and a section of a pineapple crown for a tail. Add raisin eyes and an apple wedge beak. Criss-crossed toothpicks are the feet. Press the ends of the toothpicks well into the cantaloupe rind.

Melon Lantern

Cut a slice from the bottom of a cantaloupe (or any melon) to make a flat sitting edge. Mark the melon in twelfths. Leave a 2-inch circle top and bottom. Remove every second wedge. Scoop out seeds and the inner section. Set a candle inside.

COCOANUTS

Cocoanut Bird Cage

Cut a cocoanut in half. Attach a cup hook to the top of the cocoanut shell and tie a string to it to hang it up.

Bird

The bird in the cage can be made from one large and one small radish. Toothpick the two radishes together. Add toothpick legs on the body. Thin slices of radish cut in triangles are the wings. Carve a slot in the top radish and insert a small nut to form the beak. Two capers are the eyes.

DRIED FRUITS

Dolls

Join an apricot and a date, (or a prune or a dried apple) to form the head and body of a doll. Halves of toothpicks are the arms and legs. Attach raisin hands and feet. Set the doll up on a base made of a slice of dried apricot. Facial features are also made of raisins.

Dried fruits of every possible kind can be
turned into novelties for placecards or table
decorations.

Peacock

Use a date or prune for the body. Thread raisins on several toothpicks and insert them in the body of the bird as the tail feathers.
Carve a beak on a dried apricot and place it on a toothpick and
insert it for the head. Complete the bird with two toothpick legs.

Giraffe

A dried pear is the body. Thread five toothpicks with raisins or
bits of dates. Parts of sucker sticks can be used for the legs and neck.
The head is a half a date or fig. Cut ears into the date with scissors.
Add a toothpick tail.

Dried fruit can also be served
in a basket made by cutting
out the middle of a marshmallow with scissors.

GOURDS

Shapely gourds can be turned into all sorts of intriguing characters.

Witch

The cape is made of a leaf of spinach or cabbage pinned in place. Draw on her face with crayon or food color and top her off with a paper hat.

Clown

Cut arms and legs from orange peel and hold them on with tacks or nails. Buttons are carrot circles. The clown's nose is a marshmallow. Use tiny marshmallows for the eyes and cut an orange peel mouth. The cap can be made by rolling a spinach leaf into a cornucopia shape and pinning it together. Tack it to the clown's head and attach a tiny marshmallow pom-pom to the tip of the clown's hat.

GRAPEFRUIT

Grapefruit Basket

Sketch with pencil on a grapefruit the lines of the basket. Draw on two bands across the top. Cut away the two side sections of grapefruit and the narrow section of fruit between the two ½-inch-wide bands. Remove all the grapefruit inside, leaving only the peel. Tie the two top bands together with a ribbon bow. The basket can be used to hold desserts, nuts or berries.

Flatten a grapefruit slightly on one side so it will sit firmly. Attach pineapple leaves as the tail. The head is a peeled radish. The pointed end of the radish forms the beak. Attach a narrow piece of lettuce leaf around the beak and under the radish head as the wattle (or leave some of the radish peel). A couple of raisins are the eyes. Three toothpicks arranged in a prong formation become each of the bird's feet. Press the toothpicks into the bottom of the grapefruit so that it stands level.

Grapefruit Turkey

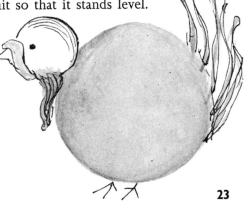

LEMONS

Alternate: *Orange or Lime*

Lemon Peel Lantern

From a large lemon, peel off a ¼-inch-wide spiral, beginning at the very top. To make it easy, mark off the spiral first with a sharp pencil and gently follow the line with a knife tip. Ease the rind away from the fruit. Ease the strip of peel back into the shape of a lemon and pin the ends so that it will stand up Insert a birthday candle inside.

Lemon Sun

For an unusual garnish, cut a slice of lemon, then cut each wedge from the peel to the middle of the lemon, being careful not to damage the peel. Turn the slice inside out so the wedges project in points. Now cut off the end of a lemon, and with a Magic Marker or with food coloring, draw on a sun face. Place the sun face inside the ring of wedges so that the points project. For a bigger display, place a half a grapefruit upside down on a plate and draw a sun face on it. Arrange the lemon wedges as rays around the sun.

Lemon Tree

Choose a stalk of celery with as many leaves on top as possible. Place it upright in a dish of cream cheese. Put half-slices of lemon on toothpicks and stick them here and there on the celery stalk.

Lemon Man

Toothpick two narrow slices of orange rind on each side of the lemon as ears. Slice a number of narrow pointed shreds of orange rind and toothpick them on for the beard and eyebrows. Pin on an unpeeled radish nose. Thin slices of radish are the eyes. With scissors, cut stars out of orange peel for the middle of the eyes. A broom straw is the lone hair.

Lemon Basket

With a pencil, draw on the outline of the basket. Cut away two sections from the top. Scallop the top leaving a band about $\frac{1}{2}''$ wide to form the handle of the basket. Remove the remainder of the lemon and use the basket to hold berries or other fruit.

MELONS

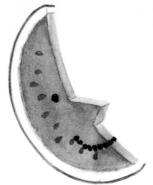

Man in
the Moon

Cut a thin, circular slice of watermelon. Cut the circle in half. Carve out the man in the moon's profile by cutting a sharp indentation towards the middle and then jutting out in a triangle to shape the nose. A maraschino cherry is the eye. Make the mouth from a number of cherry slices.

Fruit
Palette

Picturesque way to serve various kinds of fruit. Cut a 2-inch-thick slice of melon into the shape of a palette. With a spoon, cut out circles of melon all the way round the edge and fill each one with brightly colored fruit—blueberries, strawberries, nuts, grapes, etc.

Melon Vase

A melon shell with a glass inside it can be used to hold flowers. They can be real or vegetable flowers.

Melon Balls

Use a teaspoon to scoop out melon balls from various types of melons. After you have carved all of each melon into colorful melon balls, scallop the edges of the melon shell and serve assorted melon balls in each.

Melon Dishes

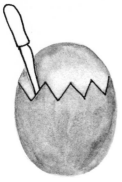

Cut a melon or cantaloupe in half in zig-zag fashion. Push a knife into the middle of the melon at an angle and pull the knife out again. Make the next cut at an opposite angle. Serve ice cream or fruit in the dish.

Melon Birthday Cake

Cut a circular slab of melon into wedges. If the melon slice is quite thick, cut the melon like a cake and stick a birthday candle on the top of each wedge. If the melon slice is about as thick as a pie, cut it in wide flat wedges and put a birthday candle on each section.

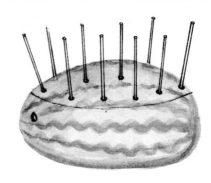

Melon Porcupine

Have a porcupine to serve the refreshments at your next party. Slice a large watermelon across, about one third from the top. Hollow out the inside of the melon. Punch small holes (large enough to hold a straw) all over the lid section of the melon. Slice off a thin piece of rind on the bottom section of the melon to make a firm base. To the front section of the base add two sunflower seeds to form the porcupine's eyes, and tack on a grape with a toothpick to form its nose. Fill the bottom melon section with ginger ale or fruit punch. Replace the top firmly and tack it in place with toothpicks. To form the porcupine's quills, put straws through the holes into the drink inside.

Slice

Flatten base

Melon lid

NUTS

The varied sizes and shapes of nuts will suggest numerous appealing creatures and all sorts of animals. Here are a few to start with:

Nut Squirrel

Glue a small chestnut on top of a large one. With scissors, cut a tail from a dried fruit, such as a date. Cut bits of dried apricot for ears, eyes, arms and feet, and glue them on to the nuts.

Nut Star

Arrange ten narrow stalks of celery all the same size in the shape of a 5-pointed star. Place the star on a platter and toothpick it together. Fill the star with assorted nuts.

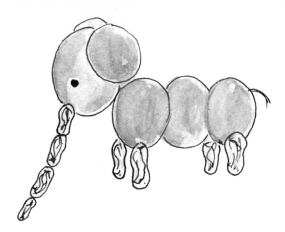

Peanut-Size Elephant

String together several peanuts to form the elephant's trunk. Attach them to a pecan or Brazil nut head. String together three more large nuts for the elephant's body and attach the head to them. Use a needle threaded with string to put the whole elephant together. Glue on four small peanuts for legs. Round slices of marshmallow can be glued on for ears. Draw on the eyes and glue on a short string tail.

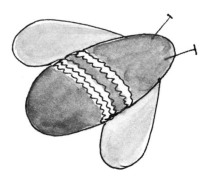

Nut Bee

A chestnut in the shell is the bee's body. Two straight pins are its antennae. Glue tiny tomato seeds around the chestnut to create the design on the bee's body. The wings are cut out with scissors from flat slices of marshmallow. Pin or glue sliced marshmallow wings to the side of the nut.

Nut Rabbit

Glue a small walnut to form the head on a large walnut. Glue on four pieces of matchsticks as the legs. A bit of peanut shell is the tail. Carve two long ears from a peanut shell and glue them in place. Draw on eyes and a nose. The rabbit can be made from either unshelled walnuts or from shells that have been glued back together again.

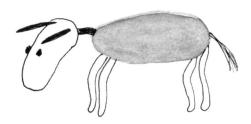

Nutty Donkey

A long unshelled peanut can be used to form the body of the donkey. His head is a Brazil nut or a large cashew nut. Use a nail to press a hole in both the peanut and the Brazil nut and then insert a part of a toothpick to hold the head to the body. Punch four more holes in the peanut and insert four slightly bent toothpicks as the donkey's legs. Glue on two long grains of rice as the donkey's ears. His eyes can be two caraway seeds.

Peanut Puppet

With a needle and strong thread, string together five peanuts in the shape of a doll. With thread, attach another round-shaped peanut for the head. Draw on eyes, nose and mouth. To make the puppet's arms and legs movable, attach a long white thread to each arm and leg and tie the threads to two fingers on each hand. By simply moving your fingers, the peanut puppet can perform tricks.

ORANGES

Alternate: Apricot or pineapple slice.

Orange Star

Cut a slice off a thick-skinned orange, about one-third of the way down. Scoop out pulp and fill with gelatin. Chill until firm. Score outer rind with sharp knife into petal shapes, and carefully peel away. White rind should be smooth and intact.

Woodpecker

Cut a thick slice from an orange and then cut it in half. Cut a section from an apple to form the base. Put two toothpicks into the apple and into the end of the orange slice to form the bird's legs. Use a thick, round slice from a carrot to make the bird's head and toothpick it into place. The pointed end of a carrot can be the woodpecker's beak.

Orange Sachets

Cover entire oranges with cloves and hang them on strings as party decorations. Afterwards the guests can take them home to hang in closets as sachets.

Bunny Cup

Scoop out an orange. Add raisin eyes and mouth. Attach lettuce ears threaded on toothpicks. Fill the cup with candies, etc., for a party.

Orange Snail

A slice of orange is the snail's body. To make the neck and head, use a long wide curved piece of orange peel. Toothpick the neck in place. Add a raisin eye and bits of toothpick as antennae. The neck can also be made from a banana. Slice the banana in half lengthwise and carve a slight curve into it. Cut another oval-shaped piece of banana and toothpick it on as the head.

Orange Curls

With a knife, peel an orange round and round to make long spiral curls.

PEACHES

Peach Flower

Arrange sections of a fresh peach around a walnut center. The stem is a slice of rhubarb or celery. Leaves are pieces of green pepper.

Clown

A slice of pineapple is the ruff. A peach, orange or apricot can be the head. Use a cherry for his nose. His mouth is a date. Eyes are criss-crossed bits of apple peel. Pour syrup over the top of the peach and shred cocoanut over it for long wavy hair. Otherwise use toothpicks.

PEARS

Pear Bowls

Hollow out pears and fill them with jelly, pudding or ice cream.

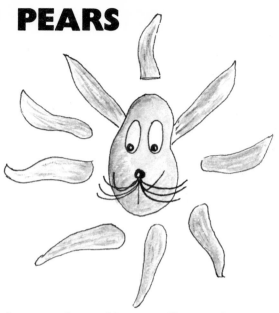

Easter Bunny

Use half a pear for the face. Put slices of banana all around the pear and attach two pieces to the small end of the pear as the rabbit's ears. Add grapes for eyes and a nose. Cut thin curly slices of orange peel for the rabbit's whiskers.

Pear Bell

For Christmas or any occasion make this bell in a jiffy. Cut off the bottom part of a pear at its widest point. Toothpick on a green or red maraschino cherry for the clapper. If it's to be a Liberty Bell, add the crack in the bell by either cutting a line in the pear with a knife or drawing on the line with food color.

PINEAPPLES

Pineapple Strawberry Barrel

Cut off the crown of the pineapple. Carefully core and hollow out the pineapple fruit about one-third of the way down. With a very sharp knife, make cuts through the skin into the pineapple on the upper side of several pineapple eyes so that these diamond shaped sections will flap downwards. Hollow out shallow depressions behind each of these eyes. Toothpick a strawberry into each hollow behind the flaps of pineapple eyes. Fill the inside of the pineapple barrel to overflowing with whole strawberries.

Pineapple Lollipop Tree

Lollipop trees can be made from either peeled or whole pineapples. To make one from a whole pineapple, simply place the pineapple in a dish and stick dried fruits, candies, cherries, etc., on to the sharp points of the leaves. Some of the dried fruit can be toothpicked in place as well.

For the other pineapple tree, first cut off the crown of leaves and carefully remove the peel. Then with a very sharp knife outline the swirls on the same angle as the pineapple eyes. Make a deep cut $\frac{1}{2}''$ from the first one and hollow out the strips of fruit to make swirled indentations all around the pineapple. Replace the crown of leaves and drape cherries in it.

Pineapple Pirate Chest

Cut off the crown of a pineapple and flatten it on one side so it will sit firmly. Cut off one-quarter of the fruit lengthwise to form the lid. Hollow out the inside. Arrange the lid on top and hold it open with toothpicks braced upright in the bottom section. Fill the pineapple treasure chest with cranberries, cherries, grapes or any brightly colored fruit.

Pineapple Punchbowl

Pineapples can be hollowed out in different ways to make attractive bowls. Cut off the crown of a pineapple, hollow out the fruit and serve soft drinks, desserts or punch in it.

Pineapple Chain

Peel the pineapple and cut it into rings or use canned pineapple slices. Cut through one side of each ring of pineapple. Slip one ring over another until you have a whole chain of them.

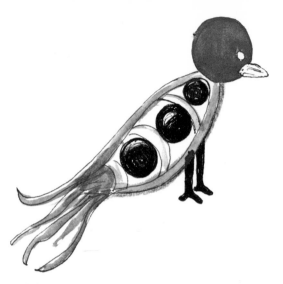

Pineapple Bird

Cut a pineapple into six pieces cutting right through the crown of leaves. Hold a wedge crust-side down to form the bird, and with a sharp knife, slice out several pieces of pineapple, being careful not to cut the strip of the core. Fill the spaces cut out with grapes or raspberries to make the bird's markings. Toothpick on a head made of a cherry. Use raisins for eyes and a nut for the beak. With a knife, cut slits in the cherry to hold the eyes and beak in place. Legs are two stiff pineapple leaves pinned in place.

PUMPKINS

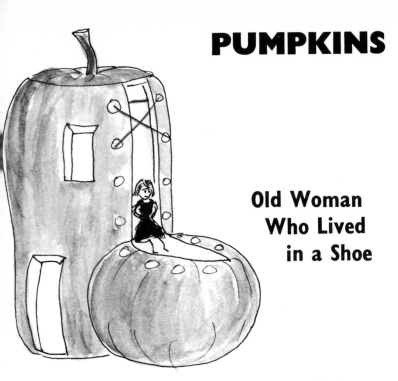

Old Woman
Who Lived
in a Shoe

Use a small round pumpkin and a long tall skinny one.
Carve off a circular lid from the tall pumpkin. Carve a long
narrow opening down the side of the tall pumpkin to the
level of the small pumpkin. On the side of the tall pumpkin
carve a window and a door. Carve a long narrow lid on the
top of the small pumpkin and remove that section. Toothpick
the small pumpkin to the tall thin one. Add cream cheese as
lace-hole-circles, and pin on string laces. The shoe house
can be filled with dolls.

Pumpkin Punchbowl

Remove the lid circle from a pumpkin and scallop the edges all the way round the opening. With cream cheese or with flour and water paste stick attractive decorative garlands around the sides of the pumpkin. Fill the pumpkin with soda pop or punch. If you have a really huge pumpkin, you can fill it with water and dunk for apples in it.

Pumpkin Globe

This unusual globe of the world can be made by gluing maps of the various continents on to the pumpkin. Copy or trace the outlines on to a piece of paper from a regular globe of the world, and cut them out. After gluing them to the pumpkin, cover them with flour and water paste to create relief maps. After the paste has dried, the continents on the pumpkin globe can be colored with vegetable coloring.

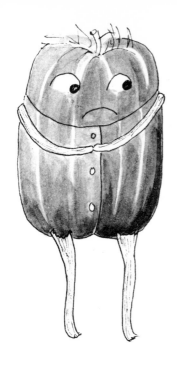

With a little artistry pumpkins can be carved or decorated to illustrate almost any classic story or nursery rhyme. With chalk, draw on the outlines of the sections to be sculpted. Carve the pumpkins with slow even strokes so that the knife does not slice past the line by accident. To begin, remove the circular lid section and clean the pumpkin very thoroughly. This will help preserve it.

Pumpkin Humpty-Dumpty

Choose a tall, thin pumpkin. Three quarters of the way up draw a line around with a Magic Marker to indicate Humpty-Dumpty's head. Draw another line straight down the middle for his suit. Toothpick on long stalks of celery for arms and legs. Cut out eyes and a mouth from cucumber rind and toothpick them in place. His buttons are tiny marshmallows pinned on. If you want your Humpty-Dumpty to have hair, a few celery tips can be pinned on top.

"Peter, Peter, pumpkin
   eater,
Had a wife and couldn't
   keep her.
Put her in a pumpkin shell
And there he kept her very
   well."

Pumpkin Prison

Carve off a round portion close to the stem and use as a lid.
After cleaning out the pumpkin, cut a window in one side of it.
Place a doll (Peter's wife) inside the pumpkin looking out of the
window. Insert several toothpicks or lollipop sticks as window
bars. Draw on the outline of a door. With food color, draw a key-
hole on to a marshmallow and toothpick it on to the door as its
padlock.

Santa Claus

Attach a small pumpkin on top of a very large pumpkin with lollipop sticks. Toothpick on a small apple for his nose and green maraschino cherries for eyes. His eyebrows are several tiny marshmallow strips pinned on. For his beard, the fur on his cap and the buttons on his suit use large marshmallows, pinned or toothpicked on. Cut arms out of paper and pin them on. Add a hat made of construction paper.

Vegetable Sculpture

Vegetables can go glamorous too. Here are a few tricks that help conjure up new vegetable shapes and personalities.

AVOCADOS

Avocado Guitar

For a unique musical instrument, try an avocado guitar. Slice an avocado pear in half lengthwise and remove the pit. Attach a stalk of celery by pressing toothpicks through it into the narrow end of the avocado. Several olives pinned to the sides of the celery near the top form the guitar's pegs. Sprinkle the avocado with lemon juice to prevent it from turning brown. You can also serve salad dressing in it.

BEETS

Beet Bike

Place two round slices of beet side by side and join them with a toothpick. Add drinking straws for the rest of the bike framework.

Beet Octopus

Can be made from celery and a beet or any round vegetable or fruit. Slice the celery into long slim strips and roll them to make them curl. Attach them to the beet with toothpicks. Add eyes made of raisins and a mouth made of a short strip of celery.

Stuffed Beets

Hollow out tiny beets and fill them with a mild blend of horseradish and whipped cream. Delicious.

Beet Boat

Scoop out the middle of a beet, and carve in the shape of a boat. Have a carrot as the mast and cut paper or lettuce leaf for the sail.

Beetnik

Choose a medium-size beet for the head. Attach carrot shreds with bits of toothpick as his beard. Cut dark glasses with scissors from a wide slice of cucumber skin and pin in place. A sliver of tomato skin is the mouth. Make his beret from cream cheese and mould it to his head. Tint it brightly with vegetable color.

Beet Cat

Arrange the beet so that the root end forms the cat's tail. Add a radish head and tack on bread ears. Use raisins for eyes and stick in whiskers made of a few straws from a broom.

Beet Turtle

Slice a beet in half. Attach four radishes as the turtle's legs and a fifth radish for the turtle's head.

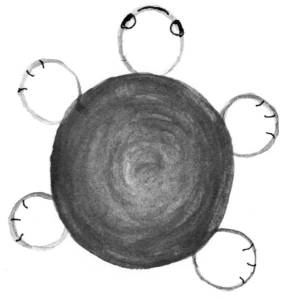

CABBAGES

Cabbage Character

Cut strips of pepper to pin on as the features. With scissors cut a collar out of a grapefruit peel. Cut the tie out of cucumber skin. The hat can be an actual hat or a hat made from grapefruit peel. Cut a long narrow strip of peel and bend it into a circle. Toothpick the ends together. Make the flat brim from a round piece of cardboard by cutting out a circle in the middle and fitting the grapefruit crown into it.

Cabbage Doll

Use a doll as the form for a vegetable dress. Hollow out the middle of a cabbage and set the doll into it up to its waist. Swirl out the leaves of the cabbage to form the doll's evening dress. Or the doll can be made out of vegetables. Toothpick on a piece of carrot to make the face and body and strips of carrot for the arms. Use corn tassels as the doll's long gold hair. Make a cherry mouth and use raisins for eyes.

CARROTS

Carrot Caterpillar

Chop up a carrot into several $\frac{1}{2}''$ sections. With a needle and string, pull the string through all the sections to make the wiggly body of the caterpillar. Attach a radish head with toothpicks, allowing two toothpicks to stick out of the head to form the caterpillar's antennae. Add a whole bunch of little raisin feet along the body of the caterpillar. Use tacks for eyes.

Carrot Telephone

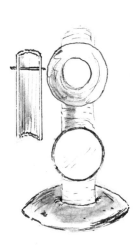

Chop off the widest parts of two big carrots and toothpick them together. Slice off a thick round piece of potato and toothpick the carrots on to this base. Slice off the rounded end of a potato about an inch thick and toothpick it at the top for the mouthpiece of the phone. A thin round slice is the dial. A length of celery is the receiver and hangs at the side on a toothpick.

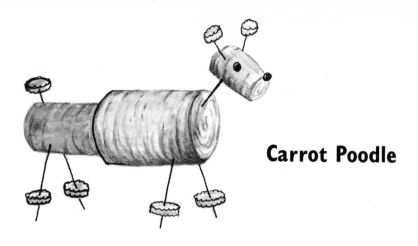

Carrot Poodle

To make the dog's pom-poms, flute the edges of a carrot by using the tines of a fork. Slice off pieces to use for the neck ruff, tail ruff and the four paws. Use part of a large carrot for the chest of the dog and attach it to a smaller section of carrot for the back quarters. Slice off a narrow piece of carrot for the head. Draw on eyes and a nose. Attach legs, neck and tail with toothpicks and slip on the circular pieces of carrot as the ruff on the legs, tail and ears.

Carrot
Curls

Start by paring a carrot crosswise. The short strip of carrot will make a small curl. Or pare lengthwise strips of carrot, roll them up and toothpick them to hold their shapes. Crisp them in ice water and remove toothpicks to serve.

Carrot Crow

To make the carrot crow, carve two small carrots into triangles. Turn the smaller one sideways and stick it on top of the larger carrot. Two olive slices are the eyes and two slices of green pepper are the spectacles. Fasten them in place with straight pins. A piece of cauliflower or broccoli is the tail. Cut a couple of carrot slices into flat triangles and attach them in place as the crow's feet.

Carrot Silverware

For the spoon, first cut the carrot in half lengthwise. Hollow out the bowl a bit, then carve the narrow handle. Make a fork the same way. To carve a knife, use the widest part of the carrot as the handle end and carve a narrow blade.

Carrot Rocket

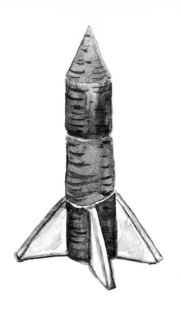

Use the widest parts of three big carrots tooth-picked together. Carve another small carrot section into a cone shape for the nose. Carve three triangles of potato and attach them at the base.

Carrot Flower

Arrange carrot slices over-lapping in a circle around an olive. Use a parsley stem.

Bowling Pins

For alley cats or for a bowling party, decorate the table with carrot bowling pins. Even off the wide end of the carrot to form the base of the pin. Carefully indent the portion above the base and round off the tips. For the bowling balls scoop out melon balls or carve a ball of carrot.

Seahorse

Carve a triangular piece of carrot for the head and attach it to the top of another carrot with a toothpick. Round out the carrot body to the shape of the seahorse. Attach a carrot curl with a toothpick as his tail. Another thin piece of carrot can be pinned to his back as the fin. Draw on the seahorse's eye with food color.

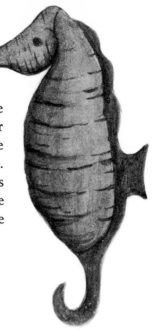

Carrot Bird

Cut a carrot in half and use the tail end as the bird's body. Toothpick on two pea pods to be the bird's wings. Paint a food color face on the bird, attach pipe cleaner feet, and wire the bird to an embroidery hoop stand.

55

CAULIFLOWER

Cauliflower Pond

Tiny cauliflowerettes taste like nuts when served raw. For a lily pond of cauliflowers separate small flower clusters from the head. Float these in a pie plate of ice water for the pond effect and also to keep them crisp. Cauliflowerettes are especially tasty topped with chip dip or cheese sauce.

Cauliflower Lion

Select a small cauliflower for the lion's head. Leave most of the green leaves around the cauliflower. They will form the lion's mane. The white part of the cauliflower will be the face. From the top half of the face, cut off a thin slice so that the upper part of the face will be recessed.

The projecting half of the cauliflower is the lion's muzzle. With a sharp knife, carefully cut in the mouth lines. Fill them with thin slivers of cucumber skin. Also glue or pin on cucumber skin for nose and eyes. Use toothpicks for whiskers.

Attach the cauliflower head with toothpicks to a cabbage or turnip body. A long piece of celery is the tail. Two more pieces of celery are the legs. Cut two thin slices of celery for the lion's feet. Slide some extra celery leaves into the cauliflower greens to fluff out the lion's ruff.

CELERY

Pale Green Witch

Bend down the uppermost stalks to form the celery witch's straggly hair. Remove all but two of the small side stalks on the piece of celery so that one branch on each side will be the witch's arms. A narrow slice of celery with some lettuce toothpicked at the bottom becomes the witch's broom.

Celery Fish

Chop a stick of celery into one-inch-long pieces. Carve each end of the pieces to a point and dab on cream cheese eyes. Use sprigs of celery tops to form the fish tails and hold them on with toothpicks. These tiny fish can be placed in the water in an ice-cube tray and frozen into ice-cubes. Each fish will then be in its own individual "ice-cube fishbowl."

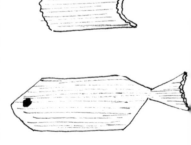

Celery Tree

Cut two stalks of celery from a bunch leaving as many branch stalks on them as possible. With thread tie the two stalks together with hollows facing to give a rounded tree trunk appearance. Set the celery in a shallow flower pot filled with earth or in a food base, such as a block of cream cheese. To the upper branches attach olives, pickles, or radishes carved into roses, etc.

Celery Curls

Make curls of celery by slicing a stalk very thin, rolling it up and letting it sit in ice water for a while to make it hold its shape.

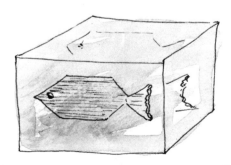

Celery Design Swirls

Clean several stalks of celery and fill with cheese. Make the stalks into a log by pressing all the cheese faces together. Tie the log to hold it in place. Slice off fairly thin coin-like pieces for an interesting shape with an unusual design.

Celery Bird

Cut off a piece of celery near the top, leaving on some of the leafy tips. Toothpick on an unpeeled radish for the bird's head. Pin on a triangle of celery for the beak and draw on eyes with food color. On small slices of carrot, draw on feet, and attach them to the bird's body with toothpicks.

NOTE: Rhubarb may be substituted for celery in all the recipes.

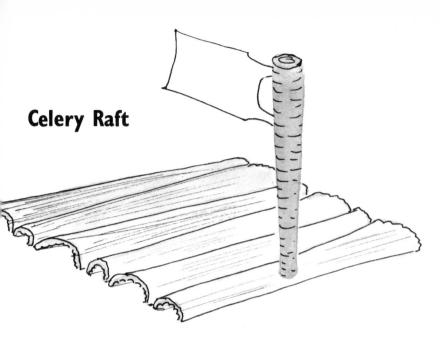

Celery Raft

Can be made of celery stalks, pickles, carrot sticks or dried corncobs. Line up several celery stalks, curved side on top, to form a rectangle. Toothpick them together. A carrot stalk is a mast. Hollow out a circle in the first celery stalk and insert the carrot tip. The shirt can be cut out of paper or from a crisp cabbage or spinach leaf. Use the raft to serve an egg or tuna fish salad.

Shrimp Boats
Are A'Comin' . . .

Fill short sticks of celery with bits of diced shrimp already mixed in a dip. Add a sail made of a smidgen of lettuce on a toothpick mast.

CORN

It's fun to transform corncobs into all sorts of novelties—from corncob pipes to corncob menageries. In addition, things sculpted or constructed from corncobs will last much longer than those made from other vegetable items.

Save the cobs after the corn has been eaten. Cut off any kernels that might still be on the cob. Dip the cobs in water to clean them off and then set them out to dry for a few days. To smooth down the texture of the parts of the corncobs which will become the faces of dolls or animals, use a piece of sandpaper or a file. Try to make the surface more even.

Carve the corncobs with a pocket knife. You may need to hammer the toothpicks into place in the cob. To make it easier, first hammer in a thin nail to make a space for the toothpick and then glue it into position.

Corncobs can be coated with lacquer or shellac to preserve them once they are carved.

Corncob Animals

Different lengths of corncob can be used to create numerous animals. Attach four lollipop sticks as legs to a corncob. Another short piece of cob is the head. Attach it to the body with a short piece of strong wire or nails. For a tail use a matchstick with cornsilk wrapped around it. Use carrots for ears and tacks for the eyes and nose.

Zombie

The plume is a lettuce leaf. Earrings and mouth are rings of orange peel. Make eyebrows and eye markings from slices of red and green peppers. The eyes are peas and the nose is a radish.

Corncob Boat

Place a cleaned and dried corncob in water for a few minutes to soften it. Bend it to get a slight curve in it. Flatten the bottom side of the cob. Insert a lollipop stick for the mast and attach a paper or cabbage sail.

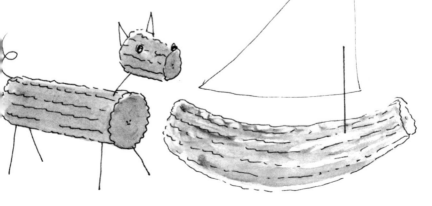

Totem Pole

Slice a turnip in half and carve a hole on the top side large enough for a corncob to stand up in. Carve notches between each head. Decorate the totem with all sorts of faces made with raisin or olive eyes, pepper slice for mouth, radish for nose, etc.

Corncob Puppets

Corncobs as well as carrots, beets, turnips or potatoes can all be turned into finger puppets. Cut off a short section of corncob. With a knife, core a hole in the bottom of the piece of

cob large enough for your finger. Paint on features. A bit of carrot can be used to carve a nose. Add hair made of cornsilk. Slip the puppet onto your finger. Cut out tiny holes for your thumb and third finger in a piece of cloth or a paper bag and put it over your hand as the puppet's costume. With a bit of imagination you will think of many more costumes for your puppets to wear. You can make animal head puppets as well and put one on each of your fingers.

Corncob Dachshund

A corncob forms the body of this unusual dachshund. Sideways slices of potato form the legs and a small potato the head. Tack on two potato chip ears with cream cheese and add a pretzel stick tail.

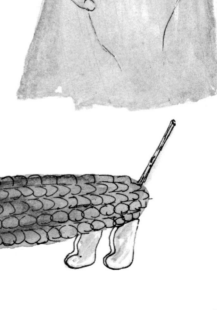

Corncob Doll

Carve an indentation on a corncob to indicate the neck. The doll is dressed in clothes made from cornhusks. Roll a cornhusk blade to make a tube. Staple it together and bend down the end of it to construct the doll's hat. Pin the hat to the doll's head. With string, tie on numerous cornhusks to make the doll's dress. Her arms can be made of leaves of corn rolled up tightly to form an arm shape. Her apron is one long leaf of cornhusk pinned to her at the neck and tied with thread around her waist. Add capers for eyes. A slice of maraschino cherry is her mouth. Make her hair of cornsilk by tying it carefully around her head.

CUCUMBERS

Cucumber Sailfish

Flatten one side of a cucumber. Cut out the fish's sail from a long, wide strip of cucumber peel. Cut a long slit in the top of the cucumber and insert the sail. Toothpick it in a couple of places to hold the sail upright. Cut a tail fin from cucumber rind, and pin it in place. Eyes are radish slices. The mouth is carved out and a slice of orange peel inserted.

Cucumber Hall of Fame

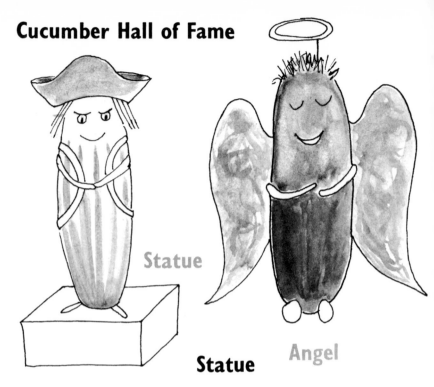

Statue

Angel

Statue

Put this famous person from history on his pedestal by tooth-picking him to a small block of cheese. Carve his hat from a circular section of orange rind and use semi-circles of the rind for arms. Color several short pieces of toothpick black and insert them into the cucumber under the hat to form his hair. His feet are little pieces of carrot. Draw on facial features with food color.

Angel

With scissors cut out wings from cabbage or spinach leaves. Slices of radish are the feet. A ring of lemon peel on a toothpick is the halo. Dab the top of the cucumber with honey and sprinkle a few carrot shreds on top for hair. Use carrot strips for the arms, and thin slivers of carrot for eyes and mouth. Carve lines for them in the cucumber and insert them into the slots.

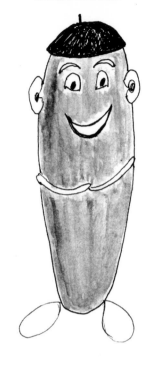

Character

Indian Squaw

Indian Squaw

Her blanket is made from a couple of cabbage leaves. Her hair is braided cornsilk. Sketch on a face with a Magic Marker, and toothpick on radish-slice feet.

Character

His beanie is the peel from half an orange. Cut features from a slice of potato. Arms can be strips of potato pinned in place, and the feet can be circular pieces of potato.

Cucumber Chain

Core a cucumber, and slice it thin. Slit one side of each piece of cucumber and loop it over another slice to form a chain.

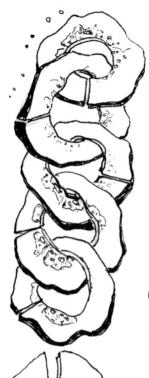

Cucumber Basket

Cut a cucumber 2 inches high. Flute the cucumber by drawing the tines of a fork over it. Cut a slice from another cucumber to form the handle and toothpick it into place.

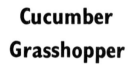

Cucumber Grasshopper

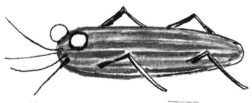

Use a small cucumber that is not too thick. Remove the rind in strips. Insert grape eyes on toothpicks. For the legs, gently bend toothpicks in half so that they do not break completely and stick them in the sides of the cucumber. The antennae can also be toothpicks, some of which are slightly bent into a curve.

LETTUCE

Old Lettuce Face

For a Lettuce Indian, tie back a few leaves of lettuce on each side to form the braids. Use a tall sprig of celery as the feather in his hair. Cut out the facial features from a pimento. Attach them with toothpicks.

Lettuce Umbrella

Use a stick of celery as the handle. With toothpicks piece together several leaves of lettuce to form a circle and toothpick the umbrella section to the celery handle.

Lettuce Holder

Hollow out a head of lettuce and use it to hold vegetables or a salad or jellied consommé.

ONIONS

Space
Critter

From outer space, this food critter can be made from an onion, potato or a pepper (red or green). Sit the pepper upright as the body. Toothpick short thin slices of orange rind on top of the pepper body as the critter's weird hair antennae. Cover the body with spots of cream cheese. The eyes are two slices of onion. Put raisin dots in the middle of them.

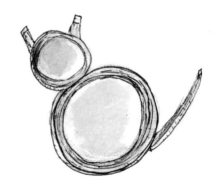

Onion Ring Cat

A witty way with onion rings turns them into a hollow white cat. A large ring is the body. Toothpick a smaller onion ring to it as the head. A strip of onion is the tail and two short triangles of onion are the ears.

Onion Mouse

To the onion body, add an unpeeled radish head and radish slice ears. Use nuts for the eyes and nose and hold them on with cream cheese. The legs are chunks of celery and the tail is a long strip of celery. This mouse may also be made from a beet with a long root.

Onion Meatballs

Carve out onions to form cups. Either put cooked meatballs into the onion cups or partially cook the meat, place in the onion cups and cook the whole thing in the oven.

PEAS

Ducklings

Baby ducks are made in minutes from peas and radishes. Cut thin slices of radish to be the duck's body. A tiny pea forms the tail and a large pea is the head. Pin them in place with straight pins. Put two pins through the head so that the heads of the pins serve as the eyes. The beak is half of a pea. Attach it with a toothpick.

Ant

A green ant is made by attaching several small peas to a straight pin. Insert tiny pieces of toothpick for the ant's legs.

PEPPERS

Pepper Bird

To a green pepper body toothpick on a tail and a wing cut from a slice of bread. Olive slices are the eyes. The legs are lollipop sticks and the feet are two radish slices.

Green Pepper Cart

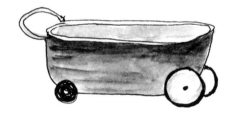

Cut a pepper in half and remove the pulp. Cut slices of carrot or radish to form the wheels. Insert the wheels with toothpicks, letting ends of picks protrude as the axle. Use a loop of long carrot strip as the handle. The cart holds radishes, celery, olives, and so on.

Pepper Holder

Slice a pepper in half and remove the seeds inside. Fill it with cream cheese or chunks of cheese on toothpicks and place on the table as a cheese dish.

Pepper Rabbit

To a green or red pepper body add a tiny onion head and onion greens for the ears. Use a piece of carrot for the tail and paws. Paint on the rabbit's face with food color.

Pepper Rings

Cut peppers round about to make circular slices. Cut the ring open and loop it around another ring to make a pepper ring chain.

PICKLES

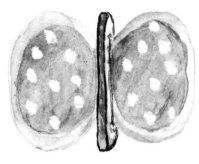

Pickle Butterfly

Use a slice of pickle for the body. Cut a deep slot into it from either side and slide a potato chip into place, one on each side, to form wings. Use dabs of cream cheese to make the spots or designs on the wings.

Fan

Make thin slices almost to the base of a pickle. Then fan the slices out.

Pickle Palm Tree

Use a stick of celery or long slim carrot for the stem. Place it in a small dish of cream cheese so that it is held quite steady. Slice small dill pickles into sections. Attach them with toothpicks in circular fashion to the top of the trunk so that they form the leaves of the palm tree.

Pickle Burro

A large dill pickle is the body. Insert four ice cream or popsicle sticks for legs and another one for the neck. Tack on a sprig of celery as the tail. Cut an end of a cucumber for the head and attach it on to the ice cream stick neck. Little triangles of cucumber skin are the ears. Make the mane with celery tips toothpicked into the head. Use a few dabs of honey to stick more celery tips to the ice cream stick neck. Use capers for eyes and nose.

Pickle Boat

Slice the bottom of a pickle to steady it. Cut out a wedge in the middle and fill with olives. Sail can be made from a thin slice of pickle on a toothpick.

POTATOES

A Noah's Ark full of animals can be made from potatoes.

Giraffe

Create a party giraffe from a potato and a few celery sticks. Carve a hole on the potato top large enough for a long piece of celery to fit into. Carve four holes on the potato bottom and insert four stiff pieces of celery for the giraffe's legs. Carve a small piece of potato in the shape of a giraffe's head and toothpick it to the celery neck. Attach raisin eyes and nose with bits of cream cheese.

Reindeer

Use a large potato for the reindeer's body and a very small one for his head. For his horns use several celery tops held in place with toothpicks. His red nose is a radish, of course. Carve tiny triangles of potato for his ears and a circle of potato for his tail. Use ice cream sticks for legs.

Piglet

This potato piglet has legs and a tail made of carrot sticks. His ears are thin pepper slices attached with toothpicks. He has corn kernel eyes and a snout made of a round slice of carrot.

Shark

Slice off a lengthwise piece from the bottom of the potato so that it will sit flat. Cut two thin triangles from a slice of potato and use one for the tail, the other for the back fin. With cream cheese attach tiny circles of potato for eyes. Carve the outline of a large shark mouth.

Owl

Slice off the bottom of a potato so that it will stand on end. From the bottom slice, carve a triangle of potato, and toothpick it on, to form the owl's beak. Add olive-slice eyes and attach small pieces of potato at the bottom for the owl's feet.

Potato Car

Carve a space in the middle of the potato to be the driver's seat. Chop seven small circles from radishes, and use four as wheels, two as headlights and one as a steering wheel.

Seal

Carve two lengthwise slices from a potato and toothpick them to the sides of another potato as the seal's flippers. Use raisins for eyes and nose. Cut so that a little white shows around the eyes.

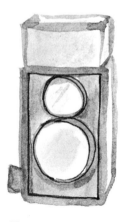

Potato Camera

Cut a potato into a rectangular shape. Slice off three different-sized circles of cucumber. Toothpick the largest circle at the bottom of the rectangle and a smaller circle near the top to form a reflex camera. Add another tiny circle of cucumber at the side as the film turner. With a knife, carve lines across the potato to indicate the viewfinder.

RADISHES

Radish Monkey

A large radish is the monkey's body. Cut a small radish in half and toothpick it on to the body with the white side for the face. A large pea forms the nose. Dots of food color are the eyes. Cut five long strips of orange peel. Two of them are the arms. One extra long strip is the tail and the two other shorter pieces of peel are the legs. Attach a small pea to each leg to form the feet.

SQUASH

Aardvark

Can be made from a squash, turnip or eggplant. If you are making this anteater from a squash or a turnip, sharpen one end of the vegetable to a point and use this pointed end as the nose. An eggplant has a natural point. Add small radishes for the feet and tail. Thin radish slices are the ears. The eyes and nose are raisins.

TOMATOES

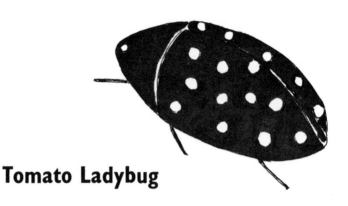

Tomato Ladybug

Cut a tomato in half. Cover three-quarters of it with cream-cheese spots to resemble a ladybug. Add a dot of cream cheese for the eye and insert several toothpicks as the legs.

Tomato Mushroom

Cut a tomato in half. Place it on a base of cucumber cut about an inch high. Cover the top of the tomato with cream-cheese spots.

Tomato Holder

Cut off the top of a tomato one-quarter of the way down from the top. Scoop out the middle of the remaining tomato. Use it to serve salmon, tuna fish, mayonnaise or mustard. Surround the tomato with endive or parsley.

Tomato Rose

First plunge the tomato into boiling water for a second to loosen the skin. Then pare the entire tomato in a spiral about $\frac{1}{8}''$ thick and 1 '' wide. Start paring with a sharp knife from the bottom of the tomato round and round towards the stem end. Be careful not to tear the peel. Wind the whole spiral of peel into a rose and fasten with a toothpick. Use a few slices of green pepper as leaves to set it on.

TURNIPS

Turnip Whale

Cut a slice off the bottom of the turnip to make a flat base. Cut out a floppy tail and two side flippers from cabbage leaves. Cut slices in the turnip to insert the tail and flippers. Use small circles of cabbage leaf for eyes and attach them with cream cheese.

Turnip Dinosaur

For this prehistoric animal's neck, use half a corncob. Toothpick it firmly in position on the turnip body. Use the other half of the corncob for the dinosaur's tail. Use a very small potato for the head and carve on eyes, nose and mouth. Cut another potato in half lengthwise and use each half for a dinosaur leg.

Turnip Elephant

Carve legs out of the turnip body. Use an onion for the head. Thin slices of potato are the ears and a carrot is the elephant's trunk.

Turnip Kangaroo

With toothpicks attach a tiny potato head and neck to the turnip body. Hollow out a pocket half way down the turnip side. Insert a radish for the head of the baby kangaroo. Use slices of a large radish for the ears. Carve two large slices of turnip for the hind legs, and toothpick them on so that they support the kangaroo upright. Add small lengths of turnip for the short upper legs. Paint features on the mother and baby kangaroo with food color.

Vegetable Flowers

Daisy

Cut narrow petals from a turnip sliced $\frac{1}{16}$" thick. For the middle cut a small round of carrot. Overlap the petals in a circle and hold the flower together with bits of toothpicks.

Pare a large, fairly white turnip, and slice into very thin circles. Roll each slice into a cornucopia. With scissors, point the tips. Slice a slim piece of carrot for the stamen. Hold all together with a straight pin or toothpick through the base. Some of the lilies can be tinted with vegetable coloring. Use parsley, mint or watercress for the leaves.

Lily

Cut and shape four petals from a turnip slice. Use a small round of green pepper for the middle. Pin the petals underneath. If desired, tint them with pink food coloring.

Dogwood

Vegetable flowers can be used in many ways. Fasten together several flowers on a doily to form a bouquet. Or tie them together with ribbons and sprinkle with sparkle dust to create a unique corsage.

Jonquil

Make from a carrot or turnip. Peel and then slice five very thin petals about 2″ x ½″. Round them with scissors. Use a slightly hollowed-out circle of carrot for the middle. Fasten together with toothpicks. Place on a green onion stem with a few more onion greens around as foliage.

Jonquil

Carrot Marigold

Hold a peeled carrot and score it lengthwise with the tines of a fork. Cut off several circles of fluted carrot and toothpick them together. Add a small pea to the top of the flower. Using a toothpick again, attach leaves made of green pepper slices.

Marigold

You can make this flower by setting a black olive on a circular slice of carrot with scalloped edges. Use a string bean for the stem, and a green pepper strip for the leaf.

Black-Eyed Susan

Carrot Sunflower

Cut long narrow petals of carrot. Cut a large circle of carrot from the wide end of a carrot. Toothpick petals around the middle circle.

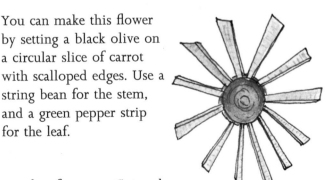

Sunflower

Poinsettia

Make red and green poinsettias from maraschino cherries. Cut each cherry into about 6 or 8 petal sections. Cut in to about $\frac{1}{8}''$ from the round end. Place the cherry on a paper towel and press it flat in the middle. Then separate out each petal to make the flower. Add leaves cut from dark cucumber skin. Serve on a square of ice cream.

Poinsettia

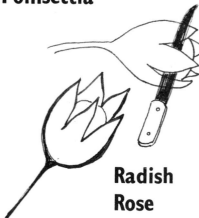

Radish Rose

Radish Rose

Do not slice off the tails of the radishes. Cut five or six thin petals around the radish. Leave a bit of red showing in between each petal. When the radishes are placed in ice water, the petals will open.

Orange Rose

Simply cut away the peel in deep scalloped petals, trying not to tear it. Begin at the stem and continue all around the orange. Continue to circle round, making scallops in several layers. Fasten the rose together with toothpicks and place on a backdrop of watercress.

Bread

Trojan Horse

To make the Trojan Horse use a small, stale sandwich loaf. For the lid, cut a one-inch-thick slice lengthwise from the whole top of the loaf. Hollow out a few inches of the inside of the bread. Fill the interior with dolls or nuts or toy prizes. Toothpick the lid back on again.

Cut four celery stalks about 5 inches long and insert them in the four corners of the loaf for the legs. (Be sure to hollow out four spaces for the celery to stick securely into the bread.) Then cut two black olives in half and toothpick each of the four sections to a leg as the horse's hoofs.

With a little imagination you will find that the contents of your bread box can take many other forms as well.

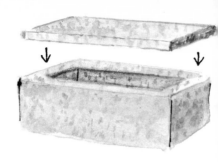

To the front end of the horse attach (again by inserting into small holes you have hollowed out) two ice cream or popsicle sticks for the neck and attach to them a small bun for the head. Two triangular pieces of bread crust are the ears. Draw on a face with food color. Wrap a length of corn-silk or yarn around the two ice cream sticks to create the horse's mane. Cornsilk can also be pinned on for his tail.

Clock

A hamburger bun easily transforms into a clock. Cut the hands out of cheese. Toothpick a gumdrop or marsh-mallow on top for the winder. Toothpick on little pieces of raisins and dates to mark off the hours.

Bun Face

On a hamburger bun place features cut from marshmallows, hard candy or vegetables.

Design Sandwiches

Spread slices of bread with peanut butter, or cream cheese and jelly. Make designs on top using chunks of pineapple or bacon strips or strips of cheese or luncheon meat.

See-Through Sandwich

Spread a slice of bread with peanut butter or some colorful filling. On another slice of bread cut a design or face right through the bread. Place the see-through slice on the other slice and the design will show through in color.

Sandwich Man

Make the face from two square slices of bread, using dried fruits to make amusing and edible features. Each ear is half a bun. The cap is a triangle of bread. Add tiny marshmallows to decorate it.

American Flag

Use a rectangle of date bread or dark bread for the background of the flag. Place on it six white stripes of wide, flat spaghetti. In the left-hand corner use white cream cheese to make the fifty white dots representing the stars. If desired, the stripes can also be made of cream cheese instead of spaghetti.

Window Box Sandwich

Cut 6 circles of bread and spread on filling to make sandwiches five layers high. Top off with a vegetable flower on a toothpick.

Champion Barbells

Made from a bread stick with a round bun on each end.

Pelican

A large hard roll is the body. A sprig of celery serves as the tail. Toothpick on a small round roll for the bird's head. To make his beak cut a round bun in half. Slice one of the halves in two pieces and use one of them for the beak. Draw on an eye with food color. Legs are two toothpicks; be sure you angle them right so the bird can stand.

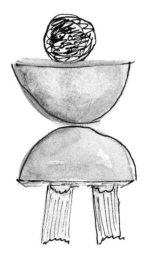

Bun Doll

Cut a hamburger bun in half. Join the two rounded sides of the bun together with toothpicks. Add celery feet and a round pickle head.

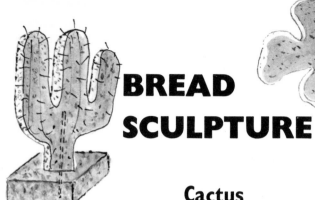

BREAD
SCULPTURE

Cactus

Plants, flowers, etc., can be cut out of bread with scissors. After cutting out the cactus, tint it green with food coloring and fasten it with a toothpick onto a thick bread slice (stale is best) to make it stand up. (See dotted line.) Dab the cactus with syrup and sprinkle a few cocoanut shreds on, to imitate the cactus' prickles.

Cup

With scissors, cut out a cup shape from a slice of bread. Open up the handle with the point of a knife. Decorate with designs cut from orange peel and pinned to the bread. Toothpick the cup from underneath to a small square of stale bread for a stand.

Bread sculpture adds a new dimension of fun to any party and is also a wonderful spare-time amusement. Bread will mould easily, like clay. When finished, it resembles foam rubber, and when stale, plastic foam.

Bun Costume

This "man" in a bun costume should be made flat to lie on a plate. Use a forked stalk of celery for the body. Place it between the two sides of a hamburger bun and toothpick it shut. The celery tips naturally form the arms and hands. The head is cut with scissors from a slice of bread and features drawn on. Toothpick the head on top of the celery body.

Bread Bonuses

For a party or just for fun, initials cut out of bread and set up on bread slices make clever placecards.

Cat

Make animals and birds from bread either by cutting them out of a slice of bread with scissors (see Cat) and standing them up with the aid of toothpicks, or sculpt the bread in three dimensions. Use very soft fresh bread.

Roll a piece of bread in your fingers till it is firm enough to be pressed into a shape. Roll various sized balls of bread to the shape needed for head, body or legs of the animal and assemble your creature with toothpicks. Features and details of costume can be pressed into the sculpture by using a matchstick or a nail file.

Make flowers by shaping small pieces of bread into petals and toothpicking them together to resemble different kinds of flower. Use wire for the stems or set them in the top of a vase.

You can even mould a set of bread chess pieces or various ornaments out of bread. It is a good material for making doll accessories and doll furniture too.

BREAD, NOODLES AND SPAGHETTI

Macaroni, spaghetti or noodles can all be used to create flat tableau pictures or unusual designs.

Trombone

Use a long piece of soft cooked spaghetti. Wind it round twice in a long loop to form the tubing of the trombone. The bell part of the instrument is made of one side of a bow-tie shaped noodle.

Baton Twirler

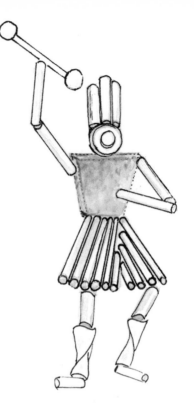

This figure can be made by sticking macaroni to cardboard with glue or syrup. The top part of her uniform is a square of bread. Her skirt is made of numerous short pieces of macaroni. A Life Saver is her head, topped off with a plumed hat made of very short pieces of a stick of spaghetti. Her arms, legs and baton are also macaroni. Her high boots are made of bow-tie shaped noodles.

Sofa

To make a genuine-looking doll sofa, cut one long narrow slice from a stale bun. Cut another short piece of bread and pin it on as the sofa's backrest. Insert four toothpicks slantwise for the legs. Better still, doll furniture can be made by moulding fresh bread into the desired shape. When it has hardened, paint the furniture with food coloring to prevent any loose crumbs from chipping off.

Eggs

Egg Flowers

Whites of hard-boiled eggs sliced into strips and placed in a circle to form petals. In the middle is an olive.

Egg Boat

Half a hard-boiled egg with a toothpick mast and a sail made of a piece of crisp bacon.

Eggs a l'Orange

Cut an orange in half across the equator and with a grapefruit knife remove the fruit. Place some cooked bacon in each of the two orange cups and drop a raw egg in on top. Sprinkle with salt, pepper and a dash of butter. Add a tablespoon of milk to prevent the yolk from shrivelling. Place the eggs in their orange cups in the oven and bake in a moderate oven (about 300° F.) about 15 minutes or till done to your taste.

Egbert, the Egg Bird

Hard boil an egg but do not remove the shell. Tape the egg with transparent tape to the bottom of a paper nut cup. Tape or glue on a marshmallow head and draw on the eyes with food coloring. Carve the beak from a gumdrop and insert with a toothpick. Tape a feather to the other end of the egg as the bird's tail feather.

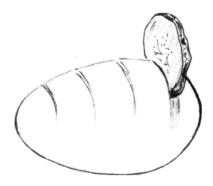

Egg
Holder

Cut slices cross-ways into a hard-boiled egg. Insert thinly sliced dill pickles, beets or carrots into each of the cuts, depending on what color your party features.

Egg Teapot

Tape a hard-boiled egg still in its shell to a nut cup. Cut a small circle of lemon rind for the teapot handle and tape it on to the end of the egg. Glue a gumdrop in the middle of the top of the egg as the top on the lid. Carve another gumdrop in the shape of the spout and glue it to the other end of the egg. With food coloring draw a design or flowers on the side of the egg.

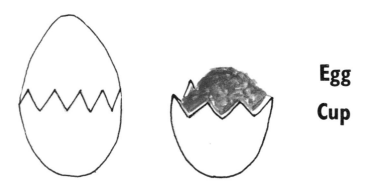

Egg Cup

Hard boil an egg, shell it and cut it in half in zig-zag fashion. This will provide two cups. Remove the yolk and fill the egg-white cups with cheese, etc.

Egg Sculpture

Carve this egghead character from a peeled hard-boiled egg. Slice a snip of egg from the bottom of the egg so it will sit steady. With a knife carefully carve a narrow slit into the yolk to form the mouth. Carve out dots of egg white to make spaces for eyes and nose. Insert unpopped kernels of corn in place as the eyes and nose.

If you wish to keep the eggs for a long time, use raw eggs, prick the ends of the shell with a pin and suck out or blow out the contents.

Egg Basket

Hard boil an egg. Slice a bit off one side of the egg so that it can be set on its side. Cut away $\frac{1}{3}$ of the egg on either side of the middle. Scoop out the yolk and use the basket to hold peanut butter or soft cheese.

Meat

Dress up any party
with these ideas
for serving meat.

Cheese Roll

Cut a long narrow stick of cheddar cheese. Roll it up in a slice of cold meat and fasten with a toothpick.

Meat Pinwheel

Take four slices of luncheon meat. Fold each kitty-cornered (see picture) and fasten with an olive on a toothpick.

Place two squares of meat flat on a plate. Connect them with a toothpick for the coupling. Slices of banana make the wheels and headlight. A small square of meat or cheese is the smokestack.

Meat Train

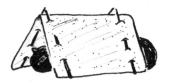

Pup Tent

Fold a square of luncheon meat in half. Thread two toothpicks on to it on each side as supports for the tent. Inside hide a small sweet pickle.

Baloney Glasses

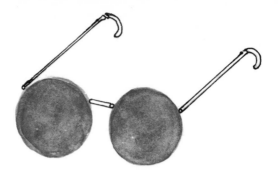

Make the eyeglasses from two circles of bologna, salami or sausage. Use uncooked spaghetti sticks as the straight parts of the frames, two small curved pieces of macaroni for the ear-pieces.

Meat Cubes

Cut luncheon meat into cubes and insert a toothpick into each cube for easy picking up.

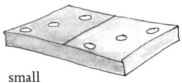

Dominoes

Cut luncheon meat into small rectangles. With a knife draw a line across the middle to resemble the line in a domino. Then add dots of cheese or circles of pimento to each rectangle of meat to form a whole set of dominoes.

Fancy Meat Rolls

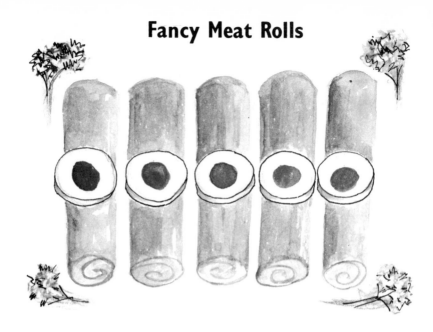

Serve slices of turkey, cold meats or ham rolled up into long cylindrical rolls. Place the meat rolls together on a platter and put a slice of hard-boiled egg on each one. Garnish the platter with endive, pickles or parsley.

Meat Loaf Stars

On each slice of meat loaf draw the outline of a star in ketchup, using a plastic squeeze bottle of ketchup to draw the decoration. Other designs can be drawn on meat slices by first cutting out a pattern on paper. Place the paper pattern over the meat and sprinkle paprika over it.

Potato Hot Dog

Hollow out the middles of small potatoes, insert a frankfurter in each one and cook them in a barbecue fire. Be sure to put them on the side of the coals away from the flames so they cook evenly and do not burn.

Mah Jongg

Cut small rectangles of meat the size of Mah Jongg tiles. Then cut long narrow pieces of process cheese or squiggles of pimento and arrange them in patterns like Chinese characters on the meat. For the Dot series of Mah Jongg cards, slices of olives can be arranged in patterns of 3 or 4 or 5, etc., on each rectangle of meat.

Cheese

Cards

Use cheese slices cut in half to form the card shape. Garnish with pieces of apple (with the skin on) cut into heart or diamond shapes. For spades or clubs, use black olives.

Cheese Hound

Two flat slices of processed cheese are the body of the dog. The legs and tail are very narrow slices of cheese. The head can be either a rectangle of meat or a different kind of cheese. Cut out a cheese triangle for the ear. Add slices of pickle for the facial features.

Cheese
Locomotive

Three overlapping square slices of cheese form the engine body. Round slices of sausage or salami are the wheels and the front of the engine. Slice a carrot in half lengthwise and use it as the smokestack. Use two small rectangles of cheese, one for the cow-catcher on the front and the other for the engineer's cab on top. A slice of carrot is the headlight. The drive shafts on the wheels are toothpicks pressed into position.

Cheese
Flower Pots

Cut cubes of cheddar cheese in the shape of square flower pots. Put a toothpick in the middle and top the toothpick with a square of cooked bacon for the leaf and an olive for the flower.

Party Ideas

The food will be the highlight of your party with some of these unique and whimsical food creations. In addition, you have found suggestions on how to coordinate the food ideas and decorations on the previous pages to set the mood for all sorts of parties.

In choosing a centerpiece, make sure that it will harmonize with the color, texture and arrangement of the rest of the foods you plan to serve. If the centerpiece is an edible one, its flavor should be suitable and fit in with the other party refreshments. Try to avoid unappetizing combinations of fruits and vegetables.

Your food sculpture will be shown off to best advantage if you don't use too many sculptured items for a single party. Choose perhaps one large item to be the centerpiece and a few small items to add variety and amusement as party favors. The simpler the arrangement, the more effective it will be. Place the centerpiece on a mirror or on top of an inverted dish to give it height on the dinner table or buffet table. Use ornaments as additional props if they fit in with the theme. Some of the food sculptures (such as various vegetable animals) can be arranged in a small tableau with perhaps a painted cardboard circus tent or jungle scene as the backdrop.

View the setting as a whole in selecting accessories to place near the carved centerpiece. If any other sculptured items are used, try to make them in proportion with one another.

For less casual parties some of the simpler ideas can be sculpted on a larger scale, or with a little inventiveness, can be adapted to create a more formal table decoration.

Once some of your guests see these centerpieces and party favors they'll want to try their hand at food sculpture too. Let them. With a bag of vegetables and a little imagination, you will create an evening's entertainment for everyone.

These party suggestions are useful for birthday celebrations, special occasions or for any day of the year. However, it is probably not advisable to combine different themes into one party.

Use your own favorite party foods as the starting point and then choose from the wide range of tasty suggestions for the following parties for ideas to add sparkle and originality to your celebration.

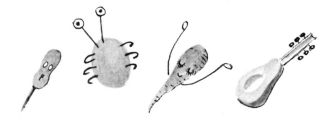

CINDERELLA'S

COACH

Set out for storyland with a few of these fanciful decorations and transform your children's party into a magic afternoon. Here are suggestions for two of the many stories you can bring to life for your young guests.

Storybook Parties

As everyone knows, pumpkins sometimes turn into beautiful fairy coaches. To have a royal coach appear on your table, first select a large, rounded pumpkin. With chalk or pencil draw a circle on top where you will cut the lid. Sketch three windows on each side of the coach. The pumpkin will look more in proportion if the outside lines of the two outer windows slant slightly towards the middle window. Draw a small triangle jutting up into the middle of the windowsill of the middle window. It will be decorated later. On the back of your coach sketch a small rectangular window, the top of which is even with the other windows. Draw a larger window on the front—perhaps with the bottom sill curved like the top of a circle.

Following your sketch lines, cut out the lid of the pumpkin. Then carefully cut out the eight windows. Clean the inside of the pumpkin. Try to get all the strings out by scraping with a spoon. On the lid only, cut or scrape off about half of the pumpkin meat to reduce the weight.

To decorate the coach, mix a paste of flour and water to a loose dough consistency. In short segments shape the paste into swirls, strips, rosettes, etc. Moisten the back of each one as soon as it is formed and stick it on to the pumpkin. Sprinkle flour on your fingers to keep the paste from sticking to them. With a little experience you will soon be able to form the paste into complicated designs.

Thick, flat slices of grapefruit are the wheels. (Or use orange slices if your pumpkin is small.) Coat these wheels with clear nail polish or shellac to preserve them and keep the juices from running out. Place toothpicks sticking straight out from the side of the coach. Pin the rind of the wheel to these toothpick axles.

The lid may be decorated with plumes, feathers or a crown. For the crown, cut out a broad, circular band of grapefruit skin. Cut wedges in the top all the way round the rind circle. Place the crown on the lid of the pumpkin.

When the party begins, light a candle inside the coach. Or (if you can) put a small transistor radio inside it for background music.

Peanut Stirrer

Draw a face on a peanut shell with food coloring. Break or cut off the tip of the shell and put the smiling peanut on the end of a swizzle stick.

Princely Sandwiches

Make grilled cheese or grilled bologna and peanut butter sandwiches. With a mustard squirter, outline a crown or a heart on the top of the sandwich.

Four and Twenty Blackbirds Pie

When this pie is opened, your guests will find hot dogs in place of blackbirds. Arrange mustard-coated frankfurters like spokes in a wheel in an unbaked pie shell. Cover with canned baked beans and sprinkle crisp bacon bits on top. Bake in a moderate oven until crust browns. At the same time, make a cover by baking an empty pie shell until golden brown and invert over pie to serve.

Cinderella Bouquet

For a delightful dessert, fill a pretty paper cup with ice cream. Stand a fancy lollipop upright in the top of the ice cream. Make two leaves by stringing green gumdrops on toothpicks. Pin a leaf into the ice cream on either side of the lollipop flower.

MAD HATTER PARTY

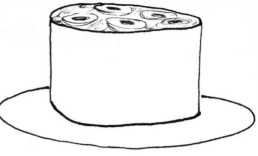

from *Alice In Wonderland*
"*Under a tree . . . the March Hare and the Hatter were having tea.*"

Your party doesn't necessarily have to be outdoors but it might be the perfect setting on a warm afternoon. Outdoors or in, here are a few ideas to help transform your guests into Mad Hatters.

Straw Hat Salad

Fill a large wooden serving bowl with fruit salad or tossed salad. Around the bottom of the bowl curve and pin together a wide band of cardboard to resemble a straw hat brim. Coat the cardboard brim with honey. Sprinkle on flakes of cereal and crushed pieces of shredded wheat to get the straw-like effect.

Top Hat Delight

A delightful centerpiece and a treat to eat! For each hat, cut five slices of bread into circles, crust removed. Spread four of these circles with jelly, peanut butter or deviled ham. Stack these slices on top of one another and put the fifth plain circle of bread on top. Cover the entire stack, top and sides with cream cheese, spread on like icing. (Soften and blend the cheese first with cream or milk to make spreading easier.) Tint a band of the cheese all round the lower edge to resemble a hat band. Place the finished stack of sandwiches on a wide brim of colored cardboard.

116

Hatters Gone Mad

Ask your guests to bring at least one old worn-out hat, explaining that everyone will create a hat at this party. Set out a supply of raw vegetables—celery, potatoes, radishes, cabbages, string beans, etc.—to decorate the hats. Then provide plenty of paste, string, blunt scissors, wire, toothpicks and used matchsticks. Give prizes for the most beautiful hat—and the "maddest." The guests must wear their hats to "tea."

Ice Cream with a Hat On

Make these ice cream clowns ahead of time in individual sauce dishes and keep in the refrigerator. For the clown's collar use a meringue or pastry ring or a large flat cookie. On this, place a round scoop of ice cream for the clown's head. Push a red gumdrop into the ice cream for the nose. Use tiny candy hearts for eyes and a sliver of licorice for the mouth. For a hat, set an ice cream cone upside down on the clown's head. Just before serving, pour chocolate syrup in the dish around the meringue or pastry base.

JUNGLE PARTY

For a swinging safari through the jungle, here are more ideas for decorating with foods. Easiest way to bag an elephant is to start with a turnip. (See page 87.) More jungle animals to use as placecards, favors or part of a centerpiece can be found on page 83 (Monkey), page 21 (Giraffe), etc.

Dessert on a Sword

Clip open a coat hanger and stretch it out into a long sword shape. To make your kabob dessert, attach marshmallows and all sorts of dried fruits, from dates to apricots to dried pears to raisins or maraschino cherries. To go with dessert, serve cookies in animal shapes.

Jungle Huts

Go native with your own grass huts. They are made in a jiffy from marsh-mallows and breakfast cereal. Dab the marshmallows with honey. Sprinkle cornflakes on the sides and bits of shredded wheat on top for the roof.

Alligator Salad

Cut off ¼ of a cucumber. This small end will be the alligator's head. The other ¾ of the cucumber will make his jaws. Cut this larger piece in half lengthwise. Then carve the alligator's jagged teeth. Toothpick the two jaws into the cut end of the head. Pin on slices of olive as his eyes. Place the alligator in a leafy green salad and arrange him so he looks as if he were surfacing through the lettuce.

Cocoanut Cannibal Mask

Use half a cocoanut shell to make this strange cannibal mask. Slice rings of lemon or orange peel and pin them on with straight pins as ear loops. Carve squares of apple peel for the eye mask and add eyebrows and a mouth cut with scissors from the skin of a cucumber.

CARTOON PARTY

Bring all children's popular cartoon characters and animals to life at this party. A whole cast of characters can move out of the comics and into three dimensions when you carve them out of vegetables. Several of these cartoon people can be used to create a centerpiece or placecards. Your guests will have even more fun converting vegetables into comic strip puppets and having them act out their lines from the funny papers.

Lying-Down-Corn-Man

He is dressed in his own cornsilk. He has circles of bread for eyes and a slice of carrot for his mouth. His arms and feet are made of bits of buns and his legs are toothpicks.

Dolls' Sandwiches

Just for fun you can serve dolls' sandwiches to go with the puppets—they are nut shells filled with cheese or peanut butter.

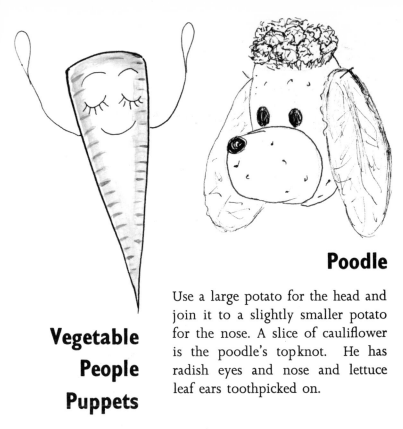

Poodle

Use a large potato for the head and join it to a slightly smaller potato for the nose. A slice of cauliflower is the poodle's topknot. He has radish eyes and nose and lettuce leaf ears toothpicked on.

Vegetable People Puppets

Give your guests all the makings of these caricature people: a sack of varied vegetables and a few beads, tacks, paper, sequins, yarn or even doll clothes. Let them draw faces on carrots and add wire arms.

Cartoon Vegetables

Other cartoon vegetables can be made by cutting out the faces of various cartoon characters and gluing them to appropriate vegetable bodies.

Tomato Star

Even a tomato is a star. Cut two circles of bread for eyes and draw a star on each one with mustard. Toothpick them on. Add slices of bread for eyebrows, nose and mouth.

Lemon Doll

Make a doll from two lemons toothpicked together. Her legs are toothpicks and her feet are gumdrops. Her arms are strips of orange peel. Add crepe paper clothes and yarn hair and draw on her face.

Pooch

Several different-sized small potatoes form this pooch. A very large potato is the chest toothpicked to a smaller potato for the hind-quarters. Attach four celery or carrot legs and four small potatoes for feet. His tail is a celery tip. He has a short carrot neck attached to two more small potatoes for head and nose. Tiny stalks of carrot with a bit of potato attached to the ends of them are his ears. Add slices of olive for eyes and draw on his nose and mouth with a Magic Marker.

HOOTENANNY

Invite your gang to gather up their ukes, banjos and records, dress up in their old clothes and shuffle over to a real old-fashioned hillbilly hootenanny.

Turnip Candle Holders

Cut turnips in half lengthwise. On the rounded side core a hole. Drip in a few drops of melted wax and insert candles to light up your hillbilly feast.

Cold Cut Banjo

Make banjo body of two slices of luncheon meat. Use celery for the top and gherkin pickle slices on toothpicks for pegs.

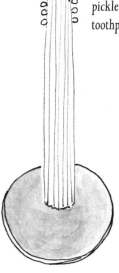

Tomato Patch Sandwiches

Slice a tomato into three sections. Spread egg salad on the middle slice and put lettuce and an onion ring on the bottom slice. Reassemble tomato into a juicy three decker sandwich.

The Skunk Who Came to Dinner

This cute table decoration is made from a turnip or an eggplant with a stem. Toothpick on a curving red cabbage leaf for a tail. From stout carrot ends, carve four legs to pin under the eggplant. Use a potato for the head with raisins for eyes and nose and nuts for ears. If your skunk is made from an eggplant, hollow out a piece of the potato and fit it over the stem to attach the head to the body. If using a turnip, a strong stick or heavy wire will pin head and body together. When the body is all assembled, paint a strip of syrup from the tip of the snout to the end of the tail and sprinkle it with shredded cocoanut to make the white stripe.

Old Smoky

The snow on top of Old Smoky is made of whipped cream. The mountain is chocolate, coffee or mocha ice cream dotted with chocolate sprinkles or ground nuts.

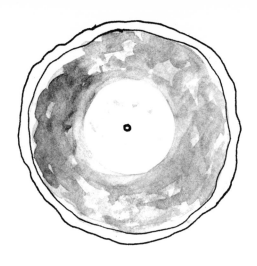

Spin-Along Pizzas

In the middle of each pizza, put circles of paper with a small hole on which you have written a Hootenanny song title—or make up your own funny titles.

Serving Suggestions

For added zing in your cold drinks, make ice cubes out of various kinds of soft drinks. Freeze cherries, raspberries, mint leaves in a few of the cubes .

Date-Nut Tracks

Side dishes can represent song titles. For "I've been Working on the Railroad" cut long strips of date-nut bread and arrange like a track on a platter. Try making up vegetable and fruit clues to other songs and have your guests guess which song they represent. For instance, the Lemon Sun, page 24, would be fine for "You Are My Sunshine."

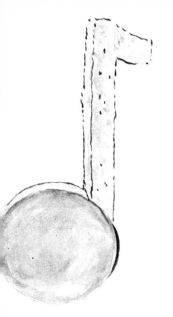

Hootenanny Notes

Add a colorful note to your party by spreading bread circles with tinted cream cheese. The crust that you have taken off the bread circles can be cut and arranged as note stems.

Hootenanny Hoot Owl

This old hoot can take its place in the middle of the table or on individual guest plates, depending on size. Make the body from a slice of ham or roast beef. Use lettuce leaves for the wings and pickle pieces for the legs and wattles. With scissors, cut the head shape from a different kind of luncheon meat or cheese. Add lemon slices with a clove in the middle as eyes, and your owl is ready to hoot.

127

SEVEN SEAS PARTY

Ship ahoy! And all aboard for a breezy change of scene. A Seven Seas party with strange and exotic dishes to tempt the laziest beachcomber and decorations to spur the imagination of any buccaneer. To set the mood, instead of a tablecloth spread a net under your catch of food—an old badminton or tennis net would be perfect.

Nutty Dugout

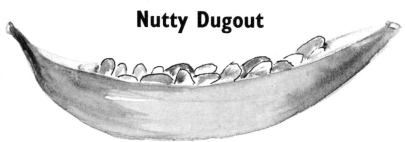

Ship Wheel

Burgers

Carefully split a banana and scoop out some of the fruit. Then load your dugout with a cargo of salted nuts.

An easy way to transform the standard hamburger and bun —arrange gherkins around the bun as wheel handles. Place a solid slice of onion on top of the roll to make the edge of the bun resemble a wheel.

Salty Suggestions

In line with the nautical theme, freeze blue cubes in your regular ice cube trays by mixing water, grape juice and a few drops of blue food coloring. If possible, serve punch or soda with these cubes in sailors' mugs or in cocoanut shells for the beach-combers in the crowd.

For other seagoing ideas, see: Egg Boat, page 100; Celery Raft, page 61; Beet Octopus, page 47; Turnip Whale, page 86; Pineapple Pirate Chest, page 39; Seahorse, page 55; Pickle Palm Tree, page 78.

Red Beard, the Pirate

Use a piece of luncheon meat for the face—bologna, turkey or roast beef. Arrange a fringe of lettuce for hair. Cut out a piece of cheese for his eye patch; a thin line of mustard will do for the string. Use small pieces of pickles for Red Beard's eyebrow and eye and a long slice of pickle for the mouth. A lemon rind ring makes his golden earring—or an onion ring if silver is your choice. Finally, shape a pointed red beard from shredded carrots and your pirate is ready to meet your guests.

Sea Side Salads

Serve fresh fruit salad mixed with tiny colored marshmallows in sea shells, scallop shells or even well-scrubbed clam shells that you have brought home from the beach. Or serve a salad of shell macaroni brightened up with bits of pimento and green pepper.

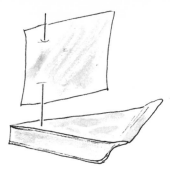

Pie Schooner

Decorate each wedge of pie with a paper or cheese sail. Rest the bottom of the cheese sail on the pie.

Submarine Sandwiches

Use long Italian loaves of bread. Push a carrot or celery stick into the top of the sandwich and affix a thick slice of stuffed olive to the top to make the submarine's periscope. Olive slices might also be toothpicked along the sides as portholes. A red maraschino cherry on the left and green on the right will serve for your port and starboard running lights.

Jellyfish Sandwiches

These add an unusual touch. Cut fish shapes from bread with a cookie cutter. Cover the bread with different kinds of jelly or alternate jelly with strips of cream cheese for an exotic striped fish. Serve open.

For this giant-size sandwich, cut 10 circles of white bread: three 4" rounds, three 3" rounds, two 2" rounds and two 1" rounds. Spread each round with butter. Cover the three bottom rounds with peanut butter and place them firmly, one on top of the other, to form the base of the lighthouse. Use tuna fish mixed with mayonnaise and chopped celery as the filling for the remainder of the rounds and pile them on top of each other in order of size.

Cut a strip of gold or silver foil to make the light on top. Form the strip into a ring and staple it. Then crumple it slightly and indent it around the middle. Place it solidly on top of the pyramid of sandwiches. Place the lighthouse on a platter. Two small sandwiches piled on top of each other can be placed at the base of the lighthouse as the lighthousekeeper's home.

Lighthouse

TOPSY-TURVY SURPRISE PARTY

"Surprise!" Not only will the guest of honor be surprised but so will all your other guests if you give a topsy-turvy party. Here's a grab bag of refreshment ideas that prove once again that appearances can be deceiving—and amusing. Topsy-turvy is a perfect party for April Fools' Day or any other day of the year.

Topsy-Turvy Sandwich

Ham on rye will be a surprise if the rye bread (a small rectangle) is hidden inside a roll of ham. Use any kind of luncheon meat or cheese slices toothpicked around the bread.

Dessert Oranges

Cut oranges in half zigzag fashion and remove the fruit. With scissors, trim the top edges of the rinds. Then fill with ice cream, sherbet or pudding. Add sauce or whipped cream and serve. If you wish, cut the oranges straight in half and conceal the sundae by placing the top half of the orange back in place before serving.

Goldfish Swallowing

This contest is sure to appeal to the younger set. With a cookie cutter, make goldfish from slices of yellow cheese, and give them capers for eyes. Float the fish in a large bowl. Give each guest a lettuce or red cabbage leaf to roll into a cornucopia-like scoop. Then stand back and see who can scoop and consume the most fish from the bowl.

Banana-Dog Hutch

Slit bananas lengthwise but do not cut through the skin on the underside. Scoop out a bit of the banana so there is room for a frankfurter to fit in. Broil franks for a few minutes until lightly browned, then insert them in the banana pockets. Place bananas with franks in a baking dish and bake in a moderate oven about 15 to 20 minutes. Slip the banana peel back as you eat.

Soup on a Stick

These colorful, nutritious soup sticks can be made from any kind of soup or combination of soups. To make a tangy tomato soupsicle, mix one can of tomato soup with one cup of tomato-vegetable juice. Add a tablespoon of lemon juice and a drop or two of Tabasco sauce. Add very thinly sliced pieces of cucumber and pour the soup into moulds. (Plastic moulds with sticks can be bought in sets. Or plastic spoons can be frozen into the soupsicles instead of sticks.) Freezing time is about three hours. After removing moulds, toothpick a lemon peel face on your soup stick.

Another popular item is the frosty chicken stick. Dissolve two chicken bouillon cubes in $\frac{1}{4}$ cup of water. Add one can of cream chicken soup and $\frac{3}{4}$ cup of milk and pour into moulds. Freezing time is about $3\frac{1}{2}$ hours. Just before serving, roll the frosty sticks in finely minced scallions or parsley.

Other Suggestions

A variety of surprise foods may be made from hard-boiled eggs. Remove the yolk and replace it with a ball of yellow cheese, marmalade, peanut butter or even a melon ball.

Edible Swizzles

A cucumber swizzle instead of a plastic one is always a pleasant surprise in punch or fruit drinks. So is a candy cane stirrer.

Illuminated Gelatin

After you have mixed the gelatin with hot water, add cold fruit juice instead of the cold water the recipe calls for. Pour into mould. When the gelatin is almost hard, place a small pocket flashlight flat on the top. Before inserting the flashlight, switch it on and cover it with a transparent wrap. To serve, simply turn the gelatin mould upside down on to a plate—or serve it on a mirror to enhance your bright idea.

Sundaes on the Half Shell

Clams for dessert will not only be a surprise but a hit as well. Concoct ice cream sundaes inside big clam shells or in large scallop shells. Put a second shell on top and seal in back with a tab of colored tape. Then wait for the surprise when your guests open their dessert. For added fun, hide a "pearl" (some small trinket) in one of the shells.

Sundae as a Side Dish

Concoct this unusual "sundae" in a sherbet or parfait dish. Use tuna fish, chicken or egg salad or even mixed greens. Top with a swirl of mayonnaise and a radish. Put less mayonnaise than usual in your salad so the topping will blend in well.

HALLOWE'EN PARTY

Apple Witch

Stick on carrot curls or cornsilk with honey as the witch's hair. The eyes, nose and mouth are slivers of cucumber skin held on with pins. The hat is made by cutting a large triangle of red cabbage or spinach leaf and rolling it to form a pointed cone. Pin the hat on. Cut another long strip of cabbage and tack it on as the brim.

Orange Pumpkin

Slice off a bit of the top of the orange and carefully scoop out the fruit inside with a parer. Carve a regular jack o' lantern in the orange skin and place a lighted birthday candle inside.

For another item see the Celery Witch on page 58.

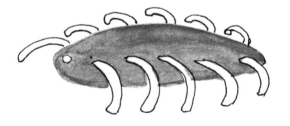

Pickle-Pede

The body is a long dill pickle. Slices of red or green pepper pinned in place are the legs. Add a raisin eye.

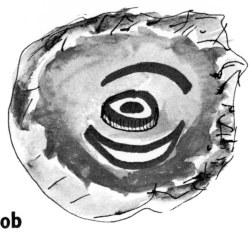

The One-Eyed Glob

A monster made of peanut butter spread on a lettuce leaf. A slice of cheese becomes his mouth and eyebrow. A slice of cucumber with a dot of radish is the monster's single eye.

Jack O' Lantern Sandwiches

Make open grilled cheese sandwiches on circles of bread. Cut triangles of pickle to make the eyes and mouth of the jack o' lantern. Serve them with "witches' brew"—(hot chocolate).

Skeleton

A skeleton can be made by using pieces of macaroni. Thread the different-size noodles on to pieces of string to form arms, legs, body and head.

Beet Bat

Carve an indentation on the top of the beet and carve the two remaining points into ears. With scissors, cut out two large wings from leaves of red cabbage. Toothpick them into place. For the bat's features, cut eyes, mouth and eyebrows out of a piece of flat cheese and pin them in place with straight pins.

Crystal Ball Dessert

For the grand finale to your Hallowe'en festivities, serve this "crystal ball" made of gelatin dessert. Mould the dessert in a large circular bowl. Just before it begins to harden, insert tiny rolled-up pieces of paper on which you have written various fortunes and strange predictions for your guests. Wrap the fortunes in foil paper first so that they will sparkle inside.

Red Pepper Devil

This red-faced devil is made from a red pepper. Cut out pointed ears from spinach, lettuce or cabbage leaves and pin them on. Carve horns from carrots or celery to be pinned on top. To make the eyes, cut triangles from marshmallows and pin in with raisin pupils. Cut strips of marshmallow for the teeth, pin them on, and outline them with vegetable coloring.

Skull and Cross-bones

Slice a radish in half. Poke two criss-cross holes in the radish one above the other and insert a length of spaghetti in each one to form the cross-bones. Add the two eyes and mouth with a black Magic Marker. If desired, you can carve the cross-bones out of carrots, and carve the features into the rounded side of the radish.

For more decorations see Pumpkins, page 41.

WINTER PARTY

Mid-winter, liven things up with a cheery party on an Eskimo theme. If your party is near Christmas or New Year's make garlands of apples, lemons, limes, etc., by stringing them on a wire and attaching in loops above doorways.

Christmas Tree Sandwiches

Use a large Christmas tree cookie cutter. Two Christmas trees can be cut from one slice of bread (be sure to avoid the crusts). Spread half of your Christmas tree slices with peanut butter, cream cheese or other filling. Then put a piece of lettuce on top. With a smaller Christmas tree cookie cutter, cut the middles out of the remaining, unspread Christmas trees. Place these outline slices over the spread slices. The lettuce will show through, making a green tree in the middle of the sandwich. If you wish, leave out the lettuce and have a show-through tree of cream cheese or egg salad.

Ice Cube Christmas Decorations

Place red and green maraschino cherries in each space in an ice cube tray, fill with water and freeze. Ice cubes with red and green cherries as ornaments are fun to serve in soda or Christmas punch.

Snowshoe Waffles

With scissors, cut waffles into snowshoe shapes. Serve with syrup, powdered sugar "snow" or piping hot under chicken a la king.

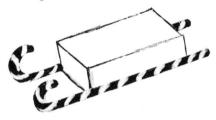

Ice Cream Sleigh

Place a square of ice cream on two candy canes so that they form the two runners of a sleigh.

Cool Cookie Column

Scrumptious way to turn cookies into a cake. Spread each cookie with whipped cream and pile one on top of another. Keep them in the refrigerator till dessert time.

Cheese Igloo

Turn a cup upside down on a saucer. Cut cheese into cubes and pile squares of cheese one on top of another all the way round the cup to form an igloo. The handle of the cup can be wrapped with a large piece of cheese to form the entrance tunnel.

For more winter party decorations, see the Seal, page 82.

Eskimo Cake Centerpiece

Decorate a round cake with a face made of icing. Place the cake on a large platter and surround it with small wedges of ice cream. Sprinkle cocoanut over the ice cream to make it resemble the fur on an Eskimo's parka.

Snowman Sandwiches

Use a round sandwich loaf to make sandwiches. Spread with your best-liked sandwich filling, then arrange the circles in twos to look like snowmen. Add raisin eyes on the top circle and raisin buttons on the bottom circle.

More Ice Cubes

Mix up separately several different powdered fruit drinks—lemonade, orangeade, etc. Pour separately into your ice cube trays and freeze them. They make colorful, tasty ice cubes for any drink.

Eggshell Igloo

Use half an eggshell. Draw on the squares of snow with pencil or crayon and color the door entrance black.

Northern Stars

Cut boiled whites of eggs into star shapes.

North Pole Sundae

Fill the middle of a doughnut with ice cream and then insert a candy cane as the pole—the North Pole.

DETECTIVE PARTY

For an exciting evening of mystery and intrigue, have a detective party. Here are a few clues to keep your amateur sleuths on the track all through the refreshments.

Private Eye Cupcake

With chocolate icing draw an eye and an eyebrow on each cupcake.

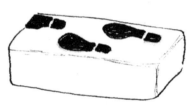

Footprint Cake

On a cake with white icing, draw big footprints with chocolate icing. Or make footprints in white on a chocolate icing. Hidden loot in the form of inexpensive prizes can also be baked into the Footprint Cake.

Handcuff Placecards

Toothpick two rings of green pepper together to resemble handcuffs. On a piece of black and white striped cardboard, write your guest's name in red and attach it to the handcuffs.

Clue Hour

Supply your guests with carrots, large potatoes and turnips that can be cut into flat slices and hold a carving contest. To give them a few ideas of things to carve, create a question mark, a pointing hand, and a big X from flat slices. To warm up, see which guest can carve the best fake moustache out of carrots. Then spread out a map of the area where the party is taking place, and have your guests compete to see who can carve the best profile map.

Sherlock Holmes Magnifying Glass

Place a doughnut on a long candy cane to make this edible magnifying glass.

The Disappearing Diamonds

Your sandwiches will certainly disappear if you serve them as a platter of diamonds. Simply shape sandwiches with a cookie cutter. Sheriffs' stars can also be made with a cookie cutter.

COWBOYS AND
INDIANS PARTY

For a Wild West party here are some party ideas, decorations and serving suggestions to delight a band of Cowboys and Indians. For the main course, serve each guest a lunch all done up in a paper bag, which they can eat anywhere along the "trail."

Cowboys will want to get their horses corralled before the Indians come after them. They can make horses from bread, page 47. Other Cowboys can clip . . . **Cowboy Boots**

. . . out of a slice of bread. Easy to do with blunt-ended scissors. The spur is bread too. For the Indians there are canoes, tepees, peace pipes and Indian beads to make.

Carrot Canoe

Use a large carrot. Flatten one side of it so it will sit flat. Round off the two ends of the carrot. Then hollow out the inside of the carrot lengthwise.

Peace Pipe

Carve a long narrow strip from a carrot. Carve the round bowl of the pipe from a piece of potato. Cut a hole in one side of the potato pipe bowl and insert the carrot stem.

Banana

Wigwam

Tie three ice cream sticks or lollipop sticks together at the top with some string. With toothpicks, attach on banana skins as the wigwam covering.

Indian Beads

Use round circles of breakfast food. Color them with vegetable coloring and string them together on a thread to form necklaces and bracelets.

Indian Tomahawks

Can be carved from vegetables or bread.

Cactus Plant

For dessert serve paper cups filled with ice cream. String several green gumdrops on to toothpicks and arrange them in the "flower pot" in the form of a cactus.

PAJAMA PARTY

Pajama Centerpiece

When the girls stay over, why not surprise them with a novel pajama centerpiece? It is made of meat, cheese and bread. Use a variety of luncheon meats, or turkey or meat-loaf slices. Arrange them on a yard-long length of wide aluminum foil in the middle of the table. Place squares of meat and cheese in two long rows to form the pajama bottoms. Butter several pieces of bread and arrange them in the shape of a pajama jacket. The night cap can be cut with scissors from two squares of cheese. The tassel is an olive.

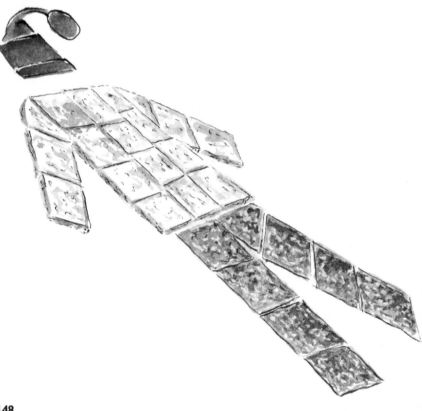

Crunchy Coiffure

For snacking during the evening, here is a unique way to serve potato chips. Spread out a square of foil wrap and put several paper table napkins on top of it. On the top napkin, draw on a girl's eyes, nose, mouth and the lower part of her face with a broad-pointed pen or pencil or lipstick. Arrange potato chips all around the face to create an extravagant hair-do. As the chips are eaten, her coiffure will undergo all sorts of hilarious rearrangements.

Noodly People

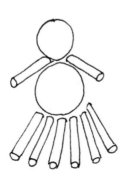

As party prizes, placecards or table decorations, noodly people are fun. They are made of different kinds of macaroni and stuck together with honey. Your guests can make a few of their own figures if they wish, and different shaped noodles can be used to create all sorts of unusual hair styles.

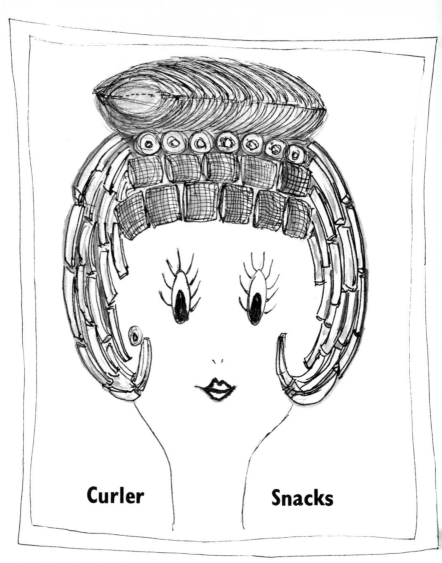

Curler   **Snacks**

Breakfast foods of various types can be served the same way as the potato chips. Draw another face on another paper table napkin and use tiny squares of shredded wheat, corn flakes, round sugar-coated cereal, and lots of tiny string potato chips. Arrange them around the face like curlers and pincurls. Use one large piece of shredded wheat for the top part of this doll's hair-set.

AEROSPACE PARTY

Foods from out of this world.

For an out-of-this-world party get off the ground with some of these aerospace ideas. To set the scene, draw runways on a paper table cloth. A rectangular cake can be iced to look like an airport hangar. A windsock can be made by cutting a marshmallow to a point with scissors and attaching it on top of the cake with a toothpick. Pear and banana planes or a turnip or eggplant helicopter can be placed on the table as a centerpiece.

Floating Prizes

"Gravity-free" party prizes and wrapped candies come floating by attached to balloons with long strings. Tie a cluster of brightly colored balloons to a ceiling fixture or to the top of a door.

Fancy drinks to liven up the festivities can be made by freezing bright red strawberries into ice cubes. Serve these specially encased space foods in soft drinks or punch.

Supply everyone with marshmallows, potatoes, peppers, assorted vegetables and gumdrops. Also put out popcorn for making eyes, ears and noses. Then let your guests' imaginations run wild as they make some strange and eerie science-fiction creatures.

Ice Cream Rocket

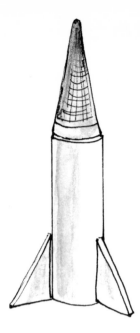

All set for the count down? Cover a tall thin glass with foil paper. Put a few ice cubes in the bottom (to fill up the glass) and a few scoops of ice cream on top. The nose cone is an ice cream cone turned upside down and set into the ice cream. Tail fins are triangular wafer cookies. (For more rockets, see page 54, carrot section.)

Astronaut

This space traveller serves up cookies and other goodies. Cut off the top of a pumpkin (or large melon) about ¼ of the way down. Scoop out the insides and carve in eyes and a mouth. Replace the top, and with a Magic Marker outline the astronaut's space helmet. Stick a couple of toothpicks on each side of the pumpkin and hang doughnuts on them as the astronaut's earphones.

Eggplant
Helicopter

Use a fairly large eggplant or turnip for the body of the helicopter. With a Magic Marker draw on the windows and door. Spread the windows with cream cheese to make them white. Attach slices of radish on the ends of toothpicks as the wheels.

Four slices of cucumber will form the propeller blades of this whirly bird. To attach them take two large wire hairpins and a small piece of carrot. Open the hairpins out flat and poke them through the sides of the carrot so that they form a criss-cross. Slide a piece of cucumber on to each of the four points. Pin the cucumber blades to the top of the eggplant with a nail passing down through the carrot section. Make the tail propeller the same way, using smaller hairpins and vegetable sections.

To suspend the helicopter you will need a needle and heavy thread. Put the thread down through the stem of the eggplant and out the lower side. Pull the thread along the underside of the helicopter and put the needle up through the front of the helicopter and out of the roof. Tie it to a chandelier or light fixture.

Banana Airplane

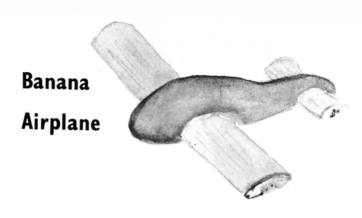

One half of a pear is the fuselage of the plane. Peel a banana and cut off ¼ of it. Slice the ¼ in half and toothpick each piece to the narrow end of the pear as tail wings. Slice the rest of the banana in half lengthwise and toothpick each piece on as the front wings.

They Came from Outer Space

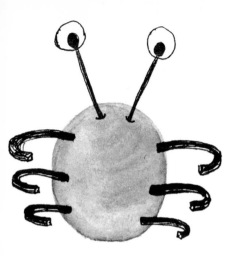

Potato Martian

Carve a slice off one end of a potato so it will sit up firmly. Cut several slices from a red pepper and attach three semi-circles of pepper on each side with straight pins as the creature's legs. Put two long toothpicks into the top of the potato and put olives on the tips of them. These are the monster's stalk-like eyes.

Two-Headed Marshmallow Monster

Toothpick three marshmallows on top of each other as the body. Add two marshmallow heads and draw on features with vegetable color. Carrot shreds stuck on with syrup form the hair. Wedges of carrot or small candies can form the feet, and long thick strips of carrot the arms.

To direct flying machines, carve traffic signs from potatoes, carrots and parsnips.

INDEX

157

158